The New Inclusion

Differentiated Strategies
to Engage *ALL* Students

The New Inclusion

Differentiated Strategies to Engage *ALL* Students

Kathy Perez

Foreword by Lim Chye Tin

Teachers College, Columbia University
New York and London

Published by Teachers College Press, 1234 Amsterdam Avenue, New York, NY 10027

Library of Congress Cataloging-in-Publication Data

Perez, Katherine D.
    The new inclusion : differentiated strategies to engage ALL students / Kathy Perez
    pages cm
    Includes bibliographical references and index.
    ISBN 978-0-8077-5482-5 (pbk. : alk. paper)
        1. Lesson planning. 2. Activity programs in education. 3. Classroom environment.
    I. Title.
    LB1027.4.P47 2013
    371.3028—dc23   2013030772

ISBN 978-0-8077-5482-5 (paper)
eISBN 978-0-8077-7261-4

Printed on acid-free paper
Manufactured in the United States of America

21 20 19 18 17 16 15 14   8 7 6 5 4 3 2 1

Contents

Foreword

I first met Kathy Perez one cold afternoon several years ago at a National Staff Development Council conference in New Orleans. I chose to attend her workshop because I was attracted by the title: "Lesson Mastery, Not Lesson Mystery." Those 2 hours warmed my heart and blew my mind, and without a second thought I invited her to come to Singapore to share her vision with our teachers. Ever since, Kathy has been coming to Singapore regularly, and hundreds of teachers here have benefited immensely from her workshops. Her insights, culled from years of experience and her own reading and research, coupled with her huge repertoire of strategies and skills, have powerfully impacted these teachers, who have brought Kathy's vision back into their own classrooms. Facilitating classroom learning the Kathy Perez way certainly makes the classroom come alive!

The most well-prepared teachers with the best-written lesson plans will affect nothing in their classrooms if the students are not engaged. Hence Kathy's approach: Students *must* be actively engaged. And if the classroom is to be an inclusive one, teachers have to recognize that their students have different learning styles and needs. In this book of *Differentiated Strategies*, Kathy shares her teaching strategies, complete with clear instruction and do-able steps to suit different learning preferences. In general, most teachers know about multiple intelligences and learning styles, but not all of them have the time or resources to customize their lessons for an inclusive classroom. This is where this book will come in as an extremely valuable resource. Kathy has helped to translate theory into practice and as teachers read and use this book, they will find themselves well on their way towards lesson mastery. On top of it all, their students will be engaged, finding their lessons meaningful and enjoyable.

—Lim Chye Tin,
Former Dean, Academy of Principals, Singapore, August 2013

Introduction

WHY DID I WRITE THIS BOOK?

I wrote this book because so many teachers in general education classrooms have not felt prepared to teach students who struggle with literacy and learning. Historically, interventions were the responsibility of trained specialists. Times have changed, and so have instructional practices. There are many schools that strive to assist and support teachers to help all students become proficient readers and writers in an inclusive setting. The Common Core Standards provide another opportunity to encourage implementation of more effective instructional practices because they promote an integrated, interdisciplinary approach to learning.

Furthermore, teaching approaches should take into account that there are many different kinds of students in every classroom and that instruction should not be limited to a one-size-fits-all approach. There are many practical strategies teachers can use to make a difference with these students who learn differently. Another reason I wrote this book with an emphasis on literacy skills is that learning to read is critical to students' academic success and has a tremendous impact on their social and emotional development as well as their achievement. "[Students] are tender individuals, easily frustrated and ashamed of deficient reading skills once they notice that many of their classmates read so effortlessly" (Lyon, 2000).

Supporting students who have difficulty learning is a pervasive challenge across all of the grade levels. For example, a fourth-grade struggling student can neither read the words nor develop meaning from the words that he *can* read in a first-grade leveled book. In another example, a high school student struggles to understand an article on photosynthesis for a research report because he has little background knowledge on the topic. These two examples highlight the need for schools to support students who struggle throughout their education. Although resource specialists, reading specialists, and literacy coaches assist, many schools and teachers need to develop techniques for use in the general education classroom to support those who struggle with literacy learning.

Additionally, many students struggling in reading and writing do not qualify for special education services because of the differing criteria used in various school districts for support programs or because of lack of sufficient funding for special support programs (Spear-Swerling & Steinberg, 1996; Wang, Reynolds, & Wahlberg, 1988). Struggling readers may or may not qualify for special education services. However, all students need effective and differentiated literacy instruction in their general education classrooms to help them succeed.

Therefore, it is important that teachers learn practical strategies for use in their inclusive classrooms that can reach all learners and boost their literacy achievement. Teachers need to learn how to design and implement effective literacy lessons that use brain-based research to maximize learning and promote student engagement. The strategies in this book will help teachers support students' unique learning styles, their cognitive and emotional needs, and their literacy development.

Furthermore, my 35 years of teaching experience as a general educator, special educator, reading specialist/literacy coach, and curriculum coordinator, along with my investigation of recent brain research, has provided me with a better understanding of powerful instructional practices that are not only essential for struggling students and students with special needs, but also benefit their peers.

The instructional tools presented in this book will help teachers face the challenges of engaging learning for struggling students and teaching in an inclusive class and make teaching more rewarding and beneficial for all students. As a former teacher and current teacher educator, I find there is a definite need for a book that offers a collection of successful techniques to intervene with struggling students. Both my graduate students and the many teachers I work with in consulting with school districts ask me to share "what works" with struggling students, "what works" to support reading in the content areas, and "what works" to support teachers in reaching their struggling students.

In reflecting on the importance of this book, one of my graduate students in education wrote to me on her culminating assignment: "Teaching is not meant to be a practice in perfection. It is an opportunity to grow, learn, ask questions and overcome challenges. Even more important, teaching exceptional students is a collaborative endeavor—to make inclusion a positive experience for all."

There are many books that help teachers support the struggling learner, and this book does that too; however, this book is unique in that it goes beyond individual teacher assistance. This book provides creative techniques that are tailored to students' learning styles to maximize the impact on their achievement in the inclusive classroom.

The continuous growth of professional educators is what I hope to encourage and nourish with this book. Teachers will have the tools to determine what works with diverse learners. They will have the information to go beyond the specific strategies described in this book to create their own brain-based strategies to promote success for all students.

KNOWLEDGE BASE

There are so many aspects to consider in an inclusive classroom. However, literacy is the key to success in school and throughout life. When I started in the profession, I was told, "All teachers are teachers of reading." This is a challenging assumption (e.g., Brozo & Simpson, 2007; Fisher & Ivey, 2006). I have broadened my thinking about literacy success to include reading, writing, speaking, listening, thinking, and communicating—encompassing all of the ways that students learn.

Therefore, all teachers need to use strategies to engage learners in all of these brain-compatible processes. This represents a significant conceptual shift from "teaching reading" to using these strategies to engage students in all of the literacy processes. My focus in this book is on research-based instructional strategies that promote learning and literacy in an inclusive classroom.

Schools traditionally assume that cognitive and academic achievement is congruent with but distinct from emotion. Respect for individual differences and sensitivity to culturally and linguistically diverse backgrounds is apparent in most schools' mission statements. However, translating that into practice and celebrating unique learning styles is not always apparent in these schools. Curriculum plans are usually based on learning specified content and developing specific skills aimed at meeting district standards. During the past decade, this approach has gained momentum and has informed educational policy and set the national educational agenda.

This same situation exists in literacy instruction in an inclusive classroom. And the practice continues in spite of an extensive body of research suggesting that students who have low reading skills also experience low self-esteem in the general education classroom (Paris, Wasik, & Turner, 1991). The research is clear that well-structured cooperative group work is one set of strategies that teachers can use to effectively meet the needs of *all* students in a heterogeneous classroom (Cohen, 1994; Johnson & Johnson, 1993; Slavin, 1989).

A common problem is that teachers haven't been empowered with high quality strategies to equip them with the sophisticated range of skills and curriculum formats necessary to get the most out of an inclusive classroom. Therefore, I will not only focus on the research regarding the importance of learning styles, differentiated instruction (Tomlinson, 2001; Gregory & Chapman, 2002), and cooperative, flexible grouping—I will also stress research-based conclusions regarding reading comprehension. This will include integration and application of the work of David Pearson (2008) regarding what works with struggling readers.

Research-based evidence supports the importance of directly teaching strategies to struggling readers. These strategies are: summarize, predict, self-question, paraphrase, clarify key issues, and create images. Time is another essential factor—time spent in actual reading. Another research-based intervention is the use of discussion. This includes dialogue with peers and adults through language-based activities.

Furthermore, research suggests that there is no perfect or best curriculum for all children with learning difficulties; however, there are several key elements to look for that virtually every research-validated curriculum that is successful with diverse students includes in some manner. These elements are found in the recent summaries of the National Institute of Child Health and Human Development (NICHD) research program concerning learning disabilities (Lyon, 2000).

In addition, little attention is given to helping teachers learn how children become proficient readers and writers. This lack of information is particularly unsettling because longitudinal studies of children who are having difficulty in learning how to read in the primary grades reveal that they struggle academically and socially throughout elementary and secondary school (Allington & Walmsley, 1995; Juel, 1988). Studies investigating student failure (Wasik & Slavin, 1993) show that literacy and learning difficulties emerge during the first years of school and that individualized instruction, provided by a knowledgeable teacher, will prevent a lifetime of failure.

As educators in inclusive classrooms, we want to support our struggling students while not letting our focus on their learning differences diminish the quality of teaching for the rest of the class. Fortunately, brain research has confirmed that strategies benefiting learners with special challenges are appropriate for engaging all learners. Understanding this brain research will increase educators' confidence in and competence with the methods that are most compatible with how students acquire, retain, and use information to become more literate.

WHAT YOU WILL FIND

The strategies that I describe throughout this book are firmly rooted in research and very practical in their application for struggling students. When teachers use and adapt these strategies to meet the diverse needs of the learners in their classrooms, they will also reach the learners at the extremes of the continuum and prevent many from "falling through the cracks" of the educational system.

The core ideas include the following:

- The most successful instructional strategies are those that teach for meaning and understanding.
- The most productive and learning-conducive classrooms are those that are student-centered and yet high in reasonable challenge.
- Students who are actively engaged and motivated will strive to meet meaningful goals and standards.

TEXT TOUR

All chapters focus on practical strategies for students who are considered struggling because they are less-able or "at-risk" readers. In addition, information for implementation and adaptation is provided to accommodate the needs of teachers at various grade levels in the inclusive classroom.

Here's a chapter-by-chapter look at what you will find in this book:

Chapter 1: Creating a Positive Environment for All Students to Learn. This chapter contains techniques for making all students feel special and welcome in the classroom. There is an emphasis on the belief that high self-efficacy is a vital component for all students to succeed in an inclusive classroom. Building a "community of learners" involves implementing strategies that allow students to support one another.

Chapter 2: Understanding the Struggling Student. Who is the struggling student in your classroom? This chapter looks at different ways children and young adults struggle with literacy across the curriculum. Teachers will learn how they can enhance the learning success of their struggling students by matching their teaching to students' learning styles.

Chapter 3: Tactile Strategies: Hands-On Learning. This chapter provides dozens of ideas for tactile learners. Hands-on strategies are described, along with adaptations for tailoring the strategies to differing ages and ability levels.

Chapter 4: Auditory Strategies: Tuning in to Literacy. This chapter offers many suggestions for modifying the curriculum to utilize strategies designed to maximize the achievement of auditory learners.

Chapter 5: Visual Strategies: The Eyes Have It for Reading. Ideas for visual learners are shared, with specific curriculum connections for various ages and abilities. Emphasis is placed on boosting visual cues in the reading process.

Chapter 6: Graphic Organizers: Making Thinking Visible. What kind of thinking will help your students to understand the critical concepts, ideas, and relationships—the "big ideas" of what they read? This chapter provides many examples of the power of graphic organizers and maps to organize thinking for struggling students.

Chapter 7: Kinesthetic Strategies: Moving on to Meaning. This chapter focuses on how to get your students physically involved in the learning process. Bring those books to life! Moving strategies increase motivation, especially for your kinesthetic learners.

Chapter 8: Common Core Standards: Navigating Text Complexity. The Common Core Standards note critical comprehension skills that students must master for success in school and in life. This chapter explores strategies for strengthening those skills. Into, through, and beyond techniques are shared. It also highlights the importance of "making it real" when it comes to strategies for struggling readers encountering informational text. Teaching implications for navigating text complexity and close reading are included as well.

Chapter 9: Curriculum Modification: Adapting Familiar Lessons. Strategies to assist students through modifications and adaptations in the classroom are covered in this chapter. Specific examples of curriculum adaptations, instructional modifications, and extension activities are included. Forms to facilitate this process in an inclusive classroom are presented as well.

Chapter 10: Managing Inclusive Classrooms to Help All Students Learn. This chapter discusses specific strategies for flexible grouping to promote achievement in an inclusive classroom. Learn practical strategies to differentiate your inclusive classroom to make your instruction more meaningful, engaging, and student-centered.

STATEMENT OF PURPOSE

This book is designed to be of practical and immediate use for you, the teacher, in your inclusive classroom. I arranged the book for easy access to the many facets of the struggling student and provide strategies to assist and support their success throughout.

There exists a plethora of possibilities with a solid knowledge base for your instructional palette. Professional practice consists of choosing skillfully from one's repertoire to match students' current circumstances and needs. I hope this book will expand your personal teaching tool kit and stimulate professional collaboration and collegial conversations to develop success for all of your students in the inclusive setting.

This book is dedicated to you, the educator. It is designed to be used by general education teachers, special education teachers, literacy coaches, staff developers, and administrators who are interested in making a difference for their at-risk readers. We, as teachers, are lifelong learners. I firmly believe that it is possible to improve student achievement by improving the way in which we teach and the way students learn. Enjoy making these strategies come to life in your classroom.

I am honored to be your guide for this journey. Thank you for selecting this book as part of your professional library. This book is also dedicated to your students—for it is for them that we enter the classroom each day.

Fasten your seat belts and let the journey begin!

CHAPTER I

Creating a Positive Environment for All Students to Learn!

THE IMPORTANCE OF A POSITIVE CLASSROOM ENVIRONMENT

Every child has the right to learn and grow in a stress-free, respectful, peaceful classroom and school. In addition, research shows that students do better both socially and academically when they feel safe and are regarded as important members of a learning community.

> Emotions and attitudes affect a child's ability to perform within the classroom. The stressful environments of both home and school can be counterproductive to learning and achievement (Southwest Educational Development Laboratory [SEDL], 2007).

It is critical for teachers, parents, administrators, and the community to strive to make each school a "caring school." Children learn and develop in many ways. One of the most important areas of growth is the development of social and emotional skills. Experienced teachers know that a classroom thrives when students feel good about themselves. Management problems decline and learning increases.

DEVELOPING SELF-EFFICACY

Many struggling students, on the surface, appear to be unmotivated or unable to learn. Teachers can strive to create a multidimensional classroom in which positive self-efficacy is fostered by recognizing that self-esteem, a sense of security, and school achievement are closely correlated. Therefore, strategies that foster a positive self-image are just as important as academic strategies to meet content standards. When teachers promote and foster social–emotional skills in their classroom, it allows the students to achieve success, both academically and with their peers. Teachers play a vital role in helping children improve in many aspects of life, including the social aspect. For struggling students, it is particularly important to instill that "can-do spirit."

Let's take a closer look at self-esteem. In his book *Educational Psychology: Theory and Practice*, Robert Slavin (2006) defines self-esteem as "the value each of us places on our own characteristics, abilities, and behaviors" (p. 80). Another way to look at it is as "belief in oneself." The way we feel about ourselves has a major effect on the way we treat others, and ourselves, and on the kinds of choices we make. Previous studies concluded that there was a positive correlation between self-esteem and academic performance. One such study found that there is a greater relationship between self-esteem and success in school than between IQ and success in school (Nave, 1990).

However, more recent studies cast doubt on the idea that higher self-esteem actually results in students doing better. Some findings even suggest that creating an artificial sense of enhanced self-esteem may negatively impact student performance (Baumeister, Campbell, Krueger, & Vohs, 2005).

An article in *Scientific American,* "Exploding the Self-Esteem Myth" (Baumeister et al., 2005), discussed how people have become consumed by their own self-esteem, with little effort to foster academic achievement or prevent undesirable behavior.

Whereas self-esteem can be perceived as a permanent internal feeling, self-efficacy is a feeling that depends upon the task or performance at hand. Self-efficacy is a concept related to self-esteem and can be fostered and developed in the inclusive classroom.

Self-efficacy was introduced by Albert Bandura (1977) and is related to locus of control and one's ability to perform a task or face a situation. Bandura (1994) described self-efficacy beliefs as determinants of how people think, behave, and feel.

Self-efficacy is a pivotal force in how students approach goals, tasks, challenges, and assignments in the classroom. Individuals with a positive sense of self-efficacy have the following characteristics:

- View challenging problems as tasks to be mastered
- Become interested in the activities they participate in
- Have a stronger sense of commitment to their interests and activities
- Have more confidence in their abilities (Bandura, 1994)

How does self-efficacy develop? These beliefs begin to form in early childhood and are strengthened through mastery experiences and social modeling in school. When students lack confidence and that "can-do spirit," teachers need to pay particular attention to their entry points of learning. This means paying attention to the students' interests, hobbies, talents, skills, and learning styles to maximize their performance in the classroom. Every year that I spent in the classroom, it was easy to identify the students with low self-esteem. They were the students who slouched in their desks, lacked confidence, and sat in the back of the room. Self-esteem is the opinion one has about him- or herself and is reflected in both behavior and performance in school.

Fostering a Growth Mindset

Many skills are required to achieve positive social development within a broad range of roles and responsibilities. Some of the most important skills to develop with your students include the ability to communicate clearly, good study habits, competent problem-solving skills, and confidence.

Fostering a growth mindset is what Dweck refers to in her book *Self-Theories: Their Role in Motivation, Personality, and Development* (2000). Teachers should focus on students' efforts, not on their abilities. Teaching a growth mindset in the classroom creates motivation and productivity (Dweck, 2006).

Why not try to have your students do their own self-efficacy check-up? When students feel good about themselves, it shows in their schoolwork, attitude, and engagement.

In fostering a growth mindset, it is important to call on students to engage them and to ensure their success. Make sure that you call on them when you know they know the answer and can succeed. This provides validation of their skills and endorses their participation in front of the peer group. You might arrange a secret signal so that students know when they are about to be called on—for instance, you might stand in a certain spot in the classroom or move closer to a specific student and put your hand on his or her desk. This gives students the necessary "heads-up" that a question is coming and gives them adequate "think time" to process the answer so that they will succeed.

The greater the sense of self-efficacy your students have, the greater the work they will produce and the more often they will succeed, and at higher levels. Give them specific praise—instead of telling them that they did a "good job," tell them what it is that they have done to make you proud. For example, if Jamal tries very hard to complete a comprehension summary assignment, tell him, "Thank you so much for working so hard on the summary." Specific praise is more powerful than generic support. In this way, the student knows in the future what behavior to repeat for positive reinforcement.

Have your students set goals for themselves and work hard to achieve them. Provide them with opportunities to reward themselves for their successes. A little attention goes a long way in the building blocks to success. Is there time during your day when you could develop their unique talents and take time for their hobbies that could be aligned with your curriculum? Allow students to spend time doing things that they are good at.

Furthermore, you need to encourage your students to avoid others who put them down. They need to respect others and treat them the way they would like to be treated. It is important to stress to students to take responsibility for their choices, actions, and accomplishments. Have the students be true to themselves and celebrate their successes. Help your students to grow in their areas of challenge and be patient with themselves.

The following tips could be posted on a bulletin board to reinforce positive behaviors. Provide these "positive pointers" to your students to enhance their sense of mastery:

- Set goals for yourself and work hard to achieve them.
- Develop your talents and take time for your hobbies.
- Reward yourself for your successes.
- Spend time doing things that you are good at.
- Ignore people who put you down or treat you badly.
- Respect others and treat them right.
- Be your own best friend—do things that are good for you.
- Make good choices for yourself.
- Spend time with caring people who like you.
- Take responsibility for yourself, your choices, your actions, and your accomplishments.
- Be true to yourself and your values.
- Celebrate your successes and plan how to grow in your areas of challenge.
- Be patient with yourself.

Affirming Activities

Have your students explore the notion of self-efficacy through writing, discussion, and reflection. These strategies not only boost their sense of self-efficacy, they also increase their writing skills, verbal and oral language skills, and socialization skills. You can adjust these assignments according to the age and/or ability levels of your students. Try some of the success-oriented assignments described in this section with your students, with modifications as necessary.

Ask your students to watch a television program and then write about one of the characters. Use the following questions and prompts: *Observe the characters personal choices. How would you describe his or her self-esteem? How can you tell? Give some examples.* This makes an excellent homework assignment and can involve the whole family. After all, the students will watch television anyway; you might as well set a positive outcome for their viewing!

Another strategy is to pose these questions to your students: *Is there something about yourself or something that you have done that you are proud of and feel good about? Why do you feel this way? What does this say about you?* In response to these questions, have each student contribute a page about him- or herself, then bind the pages together to make a "Classroom Praise Book: What Our Classroom Is Proud Of." Share some pages during Morning Message or teacher read-aloud and laminate a copy for the classroom library so that the students can read and reread about their peers. This will help build a classroom community and reinforces their reading and writing skills.

To boost your students' creativity and writing skills, as well as foster a classroom community, ask them to pretend that they are writing a letter to a future student in your class. This child is the same age that they are now. Some prompts to use for your students include: *Tell that child about yourself at this age and how you have changed since being in elementary (or secondary) school and why. Tell the student about what made you feel good about yourself and bad about yourself. Offer some advice to this student about overcoming challenges and developing that "can-do" spirit.*

Other prompts to use with a self-reflection writing activity include the following: *Having high self-efficacy means that you value yourself and what you stand for. What are things that you value most about yourself? What are some things that you do that demonstrate your self-worth? Self-perception is important for success and high self-esteem. Make a list of positive beliefs about yourself and also a list of the negative beliefs. Would your friends agree with the lists? What can you do to get rid of the negative beliefs?*

A final activity is to have each student bring in a print ad from a magazine or a hand-drawn copy of a television advertisement that is aimed at their particular age group. Lead a discussion to evaluate the ads. Some questions you might ask your students are the following:

- What assumptions does this ad make about children your age? How does this ad appeal to you?
- What is the intention of this ad? Is this ad designed to make you feel better about yourself or bad about yourself? List as many adjectives as you can that describe your feelings about this ad and its message.

All of the strategies presented here can work with students of multiple ages and grade levels. They are inclusive and success-oriented activities because there are no right or wrong answers. Try them out, and you will be amazed at the results!

Building Blocks for Boosting Self-Efficacy

The tips in this section will help to increase a growth mindset and motivation for your struggling students. Most important, you need to provide encouragement on a daily basis. For instance, put positive "sticky" notes around the classroom. Surprise your students by posting them on the classroom door as they enter or at the pencil sharpener, or even on their desks. These notes will truly encourage your students.

Why not ask your students to define the term *self-esteem?* They can draw pictures, note symbols on chart paper, or share their ideas on a team list. Help students understand the many facets of self-esteem and it how it refers to the ways we understand and value ourselves. It is important to point out to students their strengths, and to be realistic about their challenges. This is an important first step in building their self-esteem.

Look for opportunities for students to display leadership roles in class (see the resource manager tips in the "Honoring Our Students' Differences" section). Create situations where students cannot fail. Everyone likes to be a winner, and students are no different. Make time to talk alone with students. These precious moments are so meaningful to your students, and show that you value their thoughts and contributions.

Build on a child's successes—whether they are large or small. Make positive statements instead of negative ones. Find ways to give constructive criticism in a positive manner.

Another idea is to have each student make a list of "Things I Like About Me," and then add your thoughts and ideas to each list, noting the positive attributes of each student. Or, when you take attendance, instead of the students saying "here," have them say one positive thing about themselves. For instance, a student could say, "I am Judy, and I'm really good at basketball."

Call parents to tell them when their child is doing something great in class—not just when there is a problem. This kind of positive praise is important to parents and to building successful home–school relationships. Not only will this boost the student's self-concept, it will also build a positive rapport with the parents.

Involve the students as responders and thinkers, not just passive listeners. Maintain a record of successful activities. Post student work on bulletin boards. It doesn't matter what grade level you teach—this is very meaningful and rewarding for students of all ages. Try to find the best work sample for each student and post it so that everyone can see it. It is incredible how displaying students' work will increase their tendency to complete work successfully and do it to the best of their ability. In addition, maintain portfolios for each child containing their best work. Encourage parents to maintain a home portfolio with their child as well.

Involve the students in lesson presentation whenever possible; this will increase the engagement of all students in the class. Increase students' confidence by starting assignments with a few open-ended questions or activities that the students can successfully respond to. It is important to set realistic expectations so that students learn to work at their maximum potential. Stress that mistakes are positive, for they show the teacher when concepts need further review or reteaching (Nave, 1990).

Create a "Personal Graph of Greatness" with your students. On a sheet of graph paper, list the subject areas on one axis and a student self-rating scale on the vertical axis (from "need help" to "awesome"). Students then plot their own profiles to celebrate their strengths and note areas to improve. For instance, a student might rate himself "awesome" in math, and "needs help" in spelling. Have them complete these personal graphs at least two to three times a year and compare the results to note progress.

Another version of the personal profile is more open-ended and reflective in nature. In this version, students complete the following sentence stems related to school subjects:

> I like _____.
> I do not like _____.
> I am good at _____.
> I need to be better at _____.
> I am good at this subject, but I do not like it: _____.
> I am not great at this subject, but I like it: _____.

You can also design a variation of this approach and ask the students to respond to personal preferences and activities outside of school. Once again, you provide them with open-ended sentence stems. Finding out what activities the students are involved in and what motivates them can have a direct impact on their school performance as you tailor lessons to utilize these strengths and foster mastery learning. Sentence stems for this version include the following:

> I like _____.
> I do not like _____.
> I am good at _____.
> I need help with _____.
> I am good at this activity, but I do not like it: _____.
> I am not good at this activity, but I like it: _____.
> I prefer being involved in individual activities _____ or
>   group activities _____. (check one)

Furthermore, yet another version asks students to describe relationships with friends and adults. Their responses provide you, as their teacher, with another lens through which to view their self-perceptions and their interactions with others. This is helpful information when designing lessons and developing grouping strategies. In this version, students indicate "true" or "false" for statements like the following:

> I am generally well liked _____
> I am not well liked _____
> I have a large group of friends _____
> I prefer one or two friends _____
> I am a leader _____
> I am a follower _____

Here are some additional personal preferences:

> I like to eat _____.
> I do not like to eat _____.
> I relax by _____.
> I like relaxing alone _____ or with other people
> _____. (check one)

Give students time in class to complete these profiles (10–15 minutes). Ask them to take the information that they have learned about themselves and create a drawing, collage, poster, or essay showing what they learned about themselves and the different aspects of their personalities. Have them share their personal reflections with others in the class. Ask students to reflect on their responses about who they are.

Involve your students in purposeful activities to boost their self-confidence. For instance, you could have your students tutor or coach a younger child. Have them observe signs of improved self-confidence or a more optimistic outlook in their own performance as a result of helping a younger student as a peer coach.

Building a Classroom Community

Create a positive classroom learning community where students are accepted and appreciate each other. The keyword here is "community." Creating a positive learning community for your diverse learners means much more than rearranging the rows of chairs and desks. It means getting to the heart of teaching: reaching out and teaching each student—helping them "reach for the stars" by becoming stars in their own right.

It also means looking at your lesson plans with a new lens and considering how to capitalize on the strengths of each student. We need to get away from a curriculum of mere "coverage" and move toward a curriculum of *mastery*. Ask yourself, *What is it I want my students to learn, and how can I differentiate the lesson and navigate them to get there?* It is all about "lesson mastery" and not "lesson mystery." Besides building in reflection time and getting away from just "covering" material, incorporate the interactive activities in this book to promote greater collaboration among the students.

A final note is on the dilemma of bullying in our schools, which has received much attention lately. Students are not as prone to communicate "put-downs" when a curriculum of respect is integrated throughout the classroom and the school day. Make your classroom one of respect for all learners, where differences are celebrated, and put-downs are not tolerated. Learning to respect others, with their own entry points to learning, is also about honoring differences, as discussed next.

Honoring Our Students' Differences

Here are some techniques that you can learn today and use tomorrow in your classroom to promote respect and to celebrate the differences that make us unique.

Make your walls come to life with positive pitches and creative displays. Therefore, even when your students might become distracted or start to daydream, they are surrounded by "walls of wonder" that reinforce your classroom of caring. Display posters and bulletin boards that communicate your positive messages.

"Fair is not everybody getting the same thing; fair is everybody getting what they need to be successful."

"Nobody can make you feel inferior without your permission." (Eleanor Roosevelt)

An important strategy in promoting a positive classroom environment is the understanding that mistakes are acceptable.

"Mistakes happen: Take a risk!"

Have a class discussion about one or more of the preceding quotes. Ask students: *What does it mean to you? How true is it? Can you think of situations when it is not true? How does this quote reflect what you do in class?*

An excellent classroom community strategy is to create a classroom slogan and mount it on the door and around the room. Provide time throughout the week for your students to chant the slogan so that it provides them with a schoolwide classroom identity.

In addition, many books, articles, children's literature, biographies, and songs can be shared to support the positive message of accepting others. Some suggested sites for resources include the following:

www.operationrespect.org
www.teachtolerance.org

Share the positive pointers that these websites offer for helping to raise student self-esteem. Go through the lists of strategies with the students and discuss each point. Ask whether students would like to add any of their own suggestions.

Use analogies to foster understanding, either verbally or with pictures, depending on the age or ability level of the students. Some examples might include orchestra leader, doctor, coach, artist, doctor, and gardener—ask how each of these demonstrates attention to the differing needs of students.

Hold class meetings to discuss challenges and successes. Class meetings are an important part of any collaborative classroom culture—regardless of the grade level. Use the metaphor of comparing self-esteem to a bucket of water: It starts out full when we are born. However, when we develop negative beliefs about ourselves, it is like poking holes in the bucket, allowing our self-esteem to leak out. Have the group discuss things we do or say to ourselves that poke holes in the self-esteem bucket. Chart their responses and mount them on the wall as a constant reminder. As a class, discuss ways to patch up the holes and fill the bucket up again.

Give students roles and responsibilities to empower them to be leaders in the classroom community. Carefully designed procedures and routines are of paramount importance in a caring, inclusive classroom. An example of this is to randomly switch the role of "resource manager" each time table teams are used. The resource manager makes the collection and distribution of materials effective and efficient by having responsibility for these duties, and the resource manager can also be the reporter or recorder for the group during discussions and other activities. When procedures and routines such as these are adhered to, the process provides an excellent classroom management tool—things run smoothly because all resource managers know their expected responsibilities. The good news is that once the responsibilities have been established, you can use the resource manager strategy on the spot with no teacher preparation time involved.

As mentioned, you will want to rotate the resource manager selections so that all students get to fulfill the role. One way to do this is to use the following selection process:

You will be the "Resource Manager" for this activity if you are the one at your table team who:

- loves to play baseball/football/soccer/swim (etc.)
- has the birthday closest to today's date
- is the tallest/shortest member of your group

- has the fanciest footwear
- is left-handed
- has the shortest/longest/curliest hair
- has the most colorful clothes
- is wearing tennis shoes
- has freckles
- is wearing glasses
- has the most pets
- lives the farthest/closest to the school
- has the most brothers and sisters
- has the most pets (etc.)

These attributes are only a list to get you started. You will think of many more that will suit the needs and backgrounds of your students. I recommend putting individual qualities or characteristics on index cards and then randomly drawing a card—it adds to the excitement, as students are excited to see who will be selected next and what the criteria will be. This method also creates equity in the classroom, so that the same student isn't always "teacher's helper." In addition, as a result of this process, the students will experience the differences that make us unique as their differing attributes are highlighted.

Another technique that fosters honoring our differences involves, as a group, establishing norms for the classroom community. These norms would include agreeing on the conditions needed to work together, and using positive language. Post these norms on the bulletin board for all to see. You also need to discuss consequences for infractions of these norms. This might involve teaching and practicing conflict resolution techniques through role-playing as well.

Furthermore, your classroom might also include students from different cultural backgrounds and students with linguistic differences. Encourage sharing of cultural backgrounds, languages, and traditions to help celebrate the diversity in your classroom.

Working in groups. One important strategy is the use of collaborative learning. By grouping students in teams of individuals with differing ability, gender, and ethnicity, teamwork is encouraged and diversity is a strength. Collaborative learning is proven to increase self-efficacy as the group members learn to practice active listening and respect for all members (Nave, 1990). Confidence is promoted because the groups are small and flexible and each student is involved in completing the task. Achievement is also fostered as the teams work together to ensure that every member has mastered the material covered in the lesson. Collaborative learning works best after the introduction of the topic by direct instruction. Techniques for collaborative learning and flexible grouping can be found in Chapter 10.

Motivating your students. A teacher's greatest desire is to see each student motivated to learn and do well in school. Increasing school achievement is the ultimate goal for educators. This is particularly important for our struggling students. What can educators do to enhance school achievement in their students?

Setting goals. An important way to develop the intrinsic motivation to be successful is through goal setting. People, whether children or adults, will usually work harder for goals they have set for themselves than for those set by others

(Slavin, 2006). It is helpful for teachers to set up goal-setting conferences with each student on a regular basis. As the students see success in meeting their goals, their self-efficacy is positively affected. Goal-setting strategies are proven to improve academic performance (Slavin, 2006).

Offering choices. Furthermore, struggling students who are interested in what they are learning will do better. Increasing student interest can be accomplished by providing the students with choice when they are studying a concept. An example of offering students a choice is the use of "Think-Tac-Toe" activity boards. These activity boards resemble a tic-tac-toe game board, with each square featuring an assignment or activity that relates to the lesson. Students must then get tic-tac-toe by completing three activities that form a row on the board. The learning outcome of the lesson is the same for each student—to complete three of the lesson activities—but each student can choose the squares (activities) to get tic-tac-toe and to show what they understand about the lesson, concept, or unit.

There are "different ways of knowing and different ways of showing." This applies to our students and their diverse learning styles. Positive mastery learning is promoted by offering choices, as this allows students to utilize their strengths to demonstrate what they know. The students are secure in knowing that they have control over which assignments and activities they will complete.

As educators, we have a tremendous responsibility to every student who enters our classrooms, despite their differing entry points to learning. Some are highly motivated to succeed and others are not. Teachers must view students as unique individuals and celebrate the successes of all of their students.

Positive Affirmations

When recognizing the accomplishments of your students, it is important to get beyond the pedantic "very good." When they keep hearing the same praise phrase, it becomes less meaningful. They need to know specifically what they have accomplished that deserves your praise. Figure 1.1 provides a list of affirmations to expand your vocabulary to get beyond the "good" routine.

SELF-CHECK FOR TEACHERS: DEFICIT VERSUS DYNAMIC THINKING

When teaching students who may struggle with literacy processes, you may want to consider the contrast of positive (dynamic) versus negative (deficit) thinking. It is important to shift paradigms to a more positive mode for students who learn differently. Please review the checklist in Figure 1.2 and carefully reflect on the factors in each column. Where are you in your practice? Where could you be? What will you do to make a difference?

In an inclusive classroom with a diversity of learners, it is important to keep in mind and agree on the conditions needed to work together. The pointers presented here are from a teacher's perspective and reflect principles of practice that foster higher achievement in all of your students. Where do you start? What should you do?

First and foremost, you need to truly believe that *all* students can learn. The self-fulfilling prophecy is so true in education. If we don't believe they can do it, we are cutting off any opportunity to learn. However, if we believe in that "can-do

Figure 1.1. Going Beyond Just "Good" Enough—Dozens of Awesome Affirmations

Outstanding!
You're really improving.
Good remembering!
You've just about mastered that.
I'm impressed!
Nice going.
You haven't missed a thing.
Such nice work.
Nothing can stop you now!
Excellent!
That's *right*!
You are very good at that.
That's much better.
You're doing a good job.
That's it!
I knew you could do it.
Now you've figured it out.
You're learning fast.
That's the right way to do it.
You did it that time.
Wow!
Sensational!
That's the way to do it.
That's better.
That's first-class work!
Magnificent!
You're really going to town!
That's better than ever.
Now that's what I call a fine job!
You're doing beautifully!
Keep it up!
You've got that down pat!
Tremendous!
Good thinking!
Keep on trying.
Good for you!
I'm very proud of you.

That's the best you've ever done.
I'm happy to see you working so hard.
Fine!
I think you've got it now.
You figured that out fast.
That's quite an improvement
Superior work!
Keep up the good work!
Beautiful!
Congratulations.
Much better!
That's *good*!
You're on the right track now!
That's coming along nicely.
Good work!
You've just about got it!
That's a terrific job!
Wow! That's great!
Now you have it.
Super!
Nice work.
You did very well.
Right on!
Fantastic!
You're really working hard today.
I'm proud of the way you worked today.
You're doing that much better.
You're on the right track now!
That's coming along nicely.
You've just about got it!
That's a terrific job!
Wow! That's great!

Great!
Good for you!
You really make my job fun.
You're getting better every day.
Now you have it.
That's the best ever!
You must have been practicing!
Terrific!
You did a lot of work today!
You're doing fine.
You are really learning a lot.
You outdid yourself today!
Superb!
Good going!
One more time and you'll have it.
That's wonderful!
Good job, (student's name).
You remembered.
Clever!
That's great!
Well, look at you go.
Now you have the hang of it.
You've got your brain in gear today.
Wonderful!
I like the way you're working.
You make it look easy!
You really did a good job!
What neat work!
Excellent work!
You certainly did well today.
You're right!
Way to go!
Marvelous!

spirit" and give students appropriate tools and strategies to access and share knowledge, we are supporting their success. Re-ignite the passion and/or a belief in the subjects you teach. Keep in mind that, as teachers, we do not teach math or reading, we teach *children* first. It is important to know your subjects and the curriculum, of course; however, don't let a textbook or the teacher's guide dictate what gets taught.

How do we get to know our students so that we can honor all students and their learning differences? Utilize multiple measures. Do not depend on the accuracy of

Figure 1.2. How do you perceive your students?

Self-Fulfilling Prophecy (Deficit Thinking)	Proactive Thinking (Dynamic Thinking)
• He can do it. He's just not trying hard enough.	• He can do it and I will show him how.
• That's good enough. That's all I expected, considering her abilities.	• She can do better. I expect and want her to do better. I will share some strategies with her.
• He's not smart/gifted. It is useless to spend extra time with him.	• He doesn't know how to work. He needs to work on improving his effort and study skills.
• They are so lazy. They are not putting in any effort.	• They've learned poor work habits. They need clear expectations to move forward.
• She doesn't want to learn. She has "checked out."	• She has learned to dislike school (reading, etc.). How can I motivate and interest her?
• Why should I waste my time on him? He's not going to get it anyway.	• If I can't help him, I am wasting his life and time. It is my job to teach him.
• If she fails, that's her fault; that's her problem.	• If she fails, it's our fault. How can we improve? How can I meet her needs?
• I can't make a difference for those students.	• I will make a difference and reach them.

standardized tests to inform your curriculum. Informal assessment techniques need to be ongoing throughout the year. The first step to make this a reality is to gather information about students from the following sources, among others:

- Academic scores
- Interest inventories
- Personal profiles
- Interviews
- "Kid-watching"
- Learning styles
- Multiple intelligences surveys

Furthermore, spend time establishing expectations concerning respect for others, risk-taking, making appropriate choices according to individual needs, student responsibility, and student ownership of learning.

As discussed earlier in this chapter, together with your students, establish classroom norms and the conditions needed to work together and hold class meetings to address classroom concerns—as much as possible, give students ownership over the learning environment in the classroom. Finally, have appropriately high expectations and expect quality work.

You have the power to transform a student's life—use these tools wisely!

CHAPTER 2

Understanding the Struggling Student

MEET THE STRUGGLING READER

Because literacy skills are pervasive across the curriculum, and are an integral part of the Common Core Standards, this chapter focuses on strategies and interventions for students who struggle with literacy in inclusive classrooms. Struggling readers lack the essential literacy skills of proficient readers. They usually read below grade level and struggle with comprehension, phonics, and vocabulary. Feelings of defeat have turned off their desire to read. Many have adopted a "learned helplessness" attitude and may exhibit inappropriate behaviors to mask their inability to read and comprehend. Often they read very little and do not like to read. They lack effective word attack skills, have poor comprehension skills, and have limited language and vocabulary knowledge.

Let's Listen to the Students

You've probably heard comments like the following:

"I will never learn to read for the rest of my life."
"This is boring and frustrating."
"I don't understand the homework."
"I will act out, so I won't have to read."
"I am stupid—this is stupid—and you're stupid."

Out of the mouths of many struggling readers comes the same refrain: "I can't do it!" Pay attention to the frustration and angst these students feel each and every day as they encounter a page of text. Try to go beyond the obstacles and provide opportunities for these struggling students to make sense of text using the strategies that follow.

The Outlook for Struggling Students

The long-term outlook for disabled readers is mixed. The importance of early intervention cannot be understated. Teachers in inclusive classrooms can make a difference.

> Research indicates that difficulty with initial literacy acquisition may lead to less practice and motivation, and hence to continuing academic struggles. It is therefore important that these children be identified early so that they can be provided with appropriate support (Strickland, 2002).

Unfortunately, learning disabilities are not outgrown or easily overcome. Adult learning problems include slow reading rate, poor spelling, and difficulty with speech and sound skills. However, students with learning disabilities can become very skilled readers and writers and achieve success in advanced educational programs. Literacy skills continue to develop if instruction and practice are ongoing.

There is a nationwide concern about students who struggle with reading and literacy issues. If students get a poor start to reading, they rarely catch up. Research shows these students face low self-esteem, grade retention, referrals to special services, and other difficulties.

> As they progress through the grades, the curriculum marches on and the gap widens for those who do not read well (The Learning First Alliance, 1998; National Reading Panel, 1999; Rashotte, Torgeson, & Wagner, 1997; Torgeson, 1998).

CAUSES OF UNDERACHIEVEMENT IN LITERACY SKILLS

There are several causes of underachievement in reading. Why do some students struggle with reading, and what specific strategies can increase their success in an inclusive classroom?

Let's take a closer look at some examples. Many students have a lack of reading role models and enriched life experiences. These struggling readers often lack the guidance of people who can explain the purposes of reading and model the skills necessary for success: fluency, inflection, expression.

Other students may receive limited exposure to literature or Standard English vocabulary in the home. Therefore, they need to be "saturated" with abundant vocabulary in the classroom. Parent involvement is also necessary for the creation of a "print-rich" environment at home.

Many at-risk readers do not have adequate background knowledge to develop appropriate schema, and therefore struggle with the acquisition of reading skills. Teachers can help enrich background knowledge through real-life experiences, simulations, visuals, and personal storytelling.

> Direct and explicit phonics instruction is vital for struggling readers (National Reading Panel, 1999). Interventions should also include blending sounds and word patterns.

Some ideas to strengthen blending skills include classroom reviews, games that involve changing one letter to make a new word, and tapes that focus on specific sounds.

Students with poor visual processing skills might demonstrate the following indicators: difficulty with visual tracking, problems with eye–hand coordination, visual figure–ground problems, double vision, and an inability to communicate clearly what they see or don't see.

Some students with learning disabilities have difficulty with processing and memorizing information. For example, some will learn words in one context and not transfer them to the next.

All students learn unique ways of learning. Therefore, teachers need to be proactive in addressing the diverse needs of their learners. It is important to present material in many different ways, thus reaching visual, auditory, tactile, and kinesthetic learners. Pay attention to the individual learning styles of your students and provide them with diverse grouping opportunities throughout the day.

CAUSES OF COMPREHENSION FAILURE

Reading comprehension is a highly complex meaning-making process. Focusing on the causes of reading comprehension failure helps us to better understand the profile of the struggling reader and thus provide effective instruction. These causes include:

- Lack of effective comprehension strategies
- Vocabulary deficits
- Inadequate background knowledge on the topic
- Deficient word recognition skills
- Lack of awareness of different writing conventions used by authors (text features, humor, expressions, dialogue)
- Poor ability to remember and/or recall verbal information (word storage and retrieval)
- Inadequate verbal reasoning—ability to "read between the lines" (Lyon, 1998, p. 14)

Research tells us that readers who comprehend well are usually good decoders. In addition, proficient readers recognize when they do not understand and coordinate and shift the use of strategies as needed to increase their understanding.

ASSESSING THE STRUGGLING STUDENT

Warning Signals

Students who struggle with literacy may also have very diverse profiles of problems. Some may experience just one issue and others may manifest multiple symptoms that interfere with the learning process. What are some of the warning signals that a classroom teacher can look for? Here, we'll discuss at some of the core learning problems of our struggling students .

Do you have students who have an inability to manipulate individual speech sounds in words—that is, who lack phonological awareness? Or students who have difficulty with rapid naming of visual material, or visual naming speed? Also be on the lookout for students who do not use what they do know when challenged by new material. These students have not been taught strategies to use specific compensatory techniques to help overcome their difficulties and utilize their strengths.

Another warning signal is students who are unable to chunk words or chunk problems into smaller parts. These students would benefit from the use of Elkonin boxes or Unifix cubes or beads to practice putting word parts together to form a whole.

In addition, be alert for students who lack good reading-to-learn strategies. What can you do to help them "unpack" the information in the text or lesson? Stay tuned—because many more ideas to help these students follow in this book.

A common warning signal for many struggling students is spelling inaccuracy. Perhaps they have not moved beyond phonetic spelling. Many of these students have multiple transversals and reversals in their spelling patterns. Read on in future chapters for helpful strategies for addressing these types of problems.

Similarly, writing difficulties manifest themselves in students who also have spelling difficulties. Please stay tuned for techniques to try to assist and support students with writing difficulties later in this book.

Assessing Individual Differences

A powerful form of informal assessment is the use of Student Study Teams (Student Success Teams). Student Study Teams were developed as a group pre-referral process to determine from multiple perspectives the needs of a struggling student. Student Study Teams involve school-based problem-solving groups and are often the first step you should take when you have a concern about the academic progress of your students (Radius & Lesniak, 1988).

Student Study Teams are beneficial for all stakeholders: parents, general education teachers, special education teachers, school psychologists, and administrators, as well as the student (if age appropriate). The purpose of Student Study Teams is to provide a support system for students who are having difficulty in school. The team is formed within the school to examine a student's academic, behavioral, and socioemotional progress.

Careful preparation for this process is imperative. Everyone has an opportunity to share concerns and develop a plan of action. The general education teacher needs to specify accommodations and modifications that have been implemented in the classroom with the target student. The team's purpose is to seek creative ways to maximize the use of available resources and to share what is already being done for the student to assist with intervention strategies.

The parents play an important role as well. They complete an informal inventory of behaviors, interests, and strengths of the student at home and make their contributions to the meeting. This process acknowledges the sense of teamwork and facilitates the sharing of expertise.

This is a structured, facilitated process in which a wall chart that everyone is invited to contribute to is used to formulate a specific action plan. The responsibility for implementing the plan's steps is shared by everyone on the team. It is a powerful and collaborative way to address individual student needs and reduce the number of inappropriate referrals to special education. The Student Study Team provides consultation using a problem-solving approach (Radius & Lesniak, 1988) that assists in the inclusion process.

Differentiating Assessment Products

In assessing your struggling students, it is important to focus on formative assessment processes, projects, and products—instead of depending on summative measures or standardized tests—to show real growth and understanding of concepts.

The first question you might ask when you are differentiating assessment products for your students is: is it fair? What is fair? Fair is providing everyone what they need—not providing all the same thing. For example, a teacher might give a student a graphic organizer to aid in the understanding of a text. She doesn't give it to the whole class—not everyone needs it. This helps them to organize their ideas and assists studying for the test. After the lesson, the students take a traditional test on the key concepts. They all do well on the test. Is the grade fair for everyone? *Yes!* If you are differentiating your instruction, then you need to differentiate your assessment processes as well.

What does it mean to understand? What does it mean to check for understanding? In their book *Understanding by Design,* Wiggins and McTighe (2005) describe six facets of understanding that teachers need to look for and assess in all of their learners:

- Exploration
- Interpretation
- Application
- Perspective
- Empathy
- Self-knowledge

Let's take a look how we can vary assessment formats and products taking into consideration these facets of demonstrating understanding. In a differentiated classroom, it is vital to vary assessment formats to meet the needs of individual learners. There are so many different ways of knowing and different ways of showing. I want to describe some of these for you now.

In lieu of a traditional paper-and-pencil, multiple-choice, or end-of-chapter quiz, why not try something different? For instance, you could give the students a choice of few assessment options to suit their learning styles and to motivate them to respond positively. Why not offer the option to your students of demonstrating the skills that they learned to the rest of the class? They could also do a written presentation instead of an oral presentation. Another idea would be for the students to create portfolios that reflect evidence and artifacts of their learning.

Written compositions and reflections are other alternatives. This could include, for example, a 2-minute quick-write activity, or a two-word summary of key concepts. Another way to integrate writing is to use the 3-2-1 strategy. In this technique, students are asked to respond to 3 ideas they learned in the lesson, 2 ways that what they learned connects to what they already know, and 1 "I wonder" question that they have for future study. Yet another writing strategy is to have the students write journal entries to reflect on and connect the learnings of the lesson.

Students could also complete response cards to the lesson, or "exit cards," where they state key ideas learned based on prompts that you provide them. Each student needs to complete the "exit card" in order to exit the class. This is a powerful formative assessment tool because you can review these cards in less than 5 minutes to determine where the students are at—what they understand and what your next steps in the lesson need to be. Similarly, a reflective analysis is a powerful structure to use so that students can reflect on and connect the learnings or lesson material to their own lives. This can be structured as a quick-write activity and is very informative to check for understanding of the lesson.

For the visual learners, you can give them the option of creating a visual representation to display the key concepts of the lesson. For example, they could develop concept maps (described later in the book in the discussion of graphic organizers) of lesson material. In a concept map, the key concept is placed at the center and the details are represented surrounding and supporting the key concept. This is very helpful for struggling students who do not respond well to traditional note taking or constructing a linear outline. Another visual version of this summarizer technique is for the students to connect key words from the lesson, unit, chapter, or story and to be able to explain the relationships between the terms.

You can also appeal to your visual learners by having them create nonlinguistic representations to synthesize their learning, which you can then use to assess their understanding. In this method, students symbolize the content of what they are learning by drawing pictures or creating symbols, allowing them to can make sense and meaning of learning a new concept.

On the other hand, kinesthetic learners love to move to express their ideas. An easy technique to implement is carousel charts. This is a brainstorming technique that will involve all of your students in responding (Kagan, Kagan, & Kagan, 2000). First, set up several sheets of chart paper around the room. Each sheet should have a different open-ended prompt related to the lesson. You divide the students into small groups and they rotate around the room in a specific time frame to respond to each prompt. At each chart station, they first review previous ideas recorded and then add their own. After returning to their "home base" (their starting point), they review all responses from peers and select the most significant three ideas to share with the group. This keeps your students moving and responding, and helps them synthesize the material that has been covered.

In addition, kinesthetic learners love to create projects to demonstrate what they have learned from a lesson. This can involve group tasks and activities. It could also involve taking the lesson to the next step and designing an experiment to test a hypothesis.

Similarly, not only the kinesthetic learners but also all students seem to be motivated by the Frisbee or ball toss summarizer strategy. Have students form a circle or several small circles depending on the size of your class, then ask students questions about the content of the lesson. Give them the instructions: "When you catch the tossed ball, tell something important or amazing about _____, or something about _____ that you were surprised to learn."

Every pupil response is another important opportunity for informal assessment. You can provide the students with individual white boards to record their responses to a question, for example. When students are finished responding and hold them up, you can tell at a glance who has the concept and who needs further work.

An active review strategy that will help students retain information and share what they know is "Share an Idea and Get an Idea" (adapted from Kagan et al., 2000). To prepare, have the students use a list or a grid format to write down three important ideas that they learned from the lesson. Then, at the signal of motivational music playing, they are asked to mix and mingle and harvest ideas from their peers. They give an idea to a peer and then record the peer's idea on their own record sheets. They are only allowed to swap one idea with each partner and then must move on to keep the activity active. At the end of the song (music), they are asked to return to their seats. As a class, students then share what new ideas they learned from their fellow students.

Why not have your students design rubrics to showcase criteria, levels of knowledge, and understanding with teacher input and guidance? This should be a carefully modeled process. For example, you could display three student products, such as three short reflections. Then guide the students to develop criteria for exemplary, average, and unsatisfactory short responses. This will provide them with keen insight when they complete their own drafts.

Another assessment strategy choice that is active and fun is the "crumpled question toss." Students pose three questions regarding the material or lesson that has been covered. They each write these on a blank piece of paper. Then they crumple the paper like a "snowball" and gently toss it in the air for another student to catch. The student who catches the snowball needs to answer those questions. After a signal, the second student crumples it and throws it again. The student who catches it this time has to verify that the answers are correct and, if not, needs to correct them. This is a very festive and active strategy. Therefore, I recommend that this be done at the end of the class period or at the end of the day because students do get excited and zealous with this technique.

You could also utilize the "Luck of the Draw" technique, in which you present a 3- to 5-minute review of the lesson and then draw out a student's name (have student names written on index cards in a box, or on popsicle sticks in a jar) at random to determine who needs to answer the question. This adds excitement and heightens the involvement of all of your students.

Why not have your students connect to text in new and different ways? This is an excellent form of informal assessment. For instance, in a technique described by Harvey and Goudvis (2007), you first challenge your students to make text-to-text connections, relating the content to something else they have read. Next, students make text-to-student connections by connecting what they read to something in their own lives. The final phase is text-to-world, in which students make connections from the content to the world at large.

FROM DISABLED TO ABLE: TEACHING THE STRUGGLING STUDENT

It is so important to turn around the term of "disabled" to "abled." To keep that "can-do" spirit alive, think in terms of what it means to be "abled." The ABLE acronym helps describe how to keep the "can-do" spirit alive:

A = Assess
B = Build
L = Link
E = Engage

In reflecting on this acronym, ABLE, what are some ways this could help you in designing your lessons to be more inclusive of *all* learners? The process begins with careful *assessment*. It is difficult to teach without knowing each student's entry point to learning. Assessment informs instruction.

Once you have assessed the students, you are ready to *build* their skills to boost their literacy abilities. Many more tools on how to build these skills will be covered later in this book.

Next, teachers need to help struggling readers *link* their strategies for transfer of learning. This occurs with frequent modeling and demonstrating techniques so that these strategies become routine for students. Focus on strategies that good readers use. There are many examples of these techniques in this book.

Finally, *engagement* is the key for our reluctant readers. The use of brain-based techniques is essential. Lecture and "sit-and-get" techniques are not motivating for struggling students. Read on for many more ideas on how to really hook your students in the literacy-learning process.

THE POWER OF INTERVENTION

Effective reading interventions for students struggling in the early grades have been a focus of considerable research over the past 20 years (Foorman, Francis, Fletcher, Schatschneider, & Mehta, 1998; Foorman & Torgesen, 2001; Geva & Siegel, 2000; Klingner & Vaughn, 1996). Comparable research targeting older struggling students has only recently started to develop, partly in response to recent data suggesting that one in three 4th-grade students is reading below a basic level, and only 31% of 8th graders can read at the proficient level (Lee, Grigg, & Donahue, 2007).

References added

We need to assist our struggling students with a multifaceted and comprehensive literacy program. Students need systematic and direct instruction in:

- Phonemic awareness
- Phonics
- Sounding out words (decoding)
- Spelling
- Reading sight words
- Vocabulary and concepts
- Reading comprehension strategies

In addition, students need practice in applying these skills in reading and in writing. There also needs to be a focus on fluency so that the student doesn't merely "bark at print." This book is dedicated to providing many different techniques to integrate these literacy processes and to promote fluency.

Our challenge as educators is to unravel the secrets of learning disabilities that keep children shut out of literacy and learning in our classrooms (Lyon, 2000).

Struggling readers respond well to direct and explicit instruction. The following guidelines should be used as you design instruction.

First, you should address the core learning problem directly. For example, provide intensive remediation of basic speech and phonological deficits. In addition, you should provide direct instruction in basic literacy skills, with opportunities for cumulative review and repeated practice. It is important to teach students how to transfer and apply new knowledge and skills to new materials. Be explicit! Model and demonstrate positive practices provided in this book before you expect your students to do these strategies independently. Teach the strategies used by skilled readers to attack unknown words, such as comparing the unknown word to a known word, and commend them for their efforts. Have students try different vowel pronunciations—is it long or short? Ask your students to focus on prefixes and suffixes and "peel them off." Does that help them in pronunciation and understanding? Another strategy is to ask students to underline the parts of the word that they know. Then they start from there to positively decode the unknown word. Context clues are also important. Ask the student: "What makes sense in this sentence?"

Another important intervention strategy is to teach students to be flexible: try different strategies and evaluate how well they work. Have the students acknowledge their own efforts and their successes. Work on learning to read and spell the same sets of words.

Students should learn that reading can be fun. Use stories and materials that are interesting and allow for successful reading by struggling readers. Build reading comprehension skills by teaching the strategies used by good readers, as just described. Move from stories to informational texts. Then add and model the following important comprehension techniques: predicting, generating questions, clarifying, and summarizing. In addition, please try to have your students write every day. It can be as simple as writing reactions to stories read. Value the expression of individual opinions and creative approaches.

Providing a broad range of literacy experiences gives students multiple pathways to comprehension. One important pathway is through phonology and appropriate word attack skills.

PHONOLOGY AND WORD ATTACK SKILLS

Guidelines for Phonological Awareness Instruction

In this section we will look at principles of early literacy instruction for students with moderate reading disabilities.

It is important to increase the *consistency* and *redundancy* of your lesson content based upon the level of reading impairment of the student. Use the *same set of words* in the lesson for decoding in phrases, in sentences, and in a passage.

If the student is reading at a low level, teach phonological awareness to a point where the student can remember, state, and blend discreet speech sounds into a word. Students should also be able to segment speech sounds in a word using manipulatives.

Another important technique for struggling readers is to *eliminate letter confusion* (e.g., *b, d, p, z*). Address one confusing letter at a time. For example, teach *b* until the student can respond accurately to the letter–sound correspondence on a card, in text, and from dictation. Then teach *d* with the same intensity. Then combine the letters into small words on paper—for example, *bid, rib*. "Screen spelling," described later in the book, will assist with reversals and help students experience letter development in a tactile way.

Consider monitoring the level of text difficulty. When a student's accuracy goes down in reading a passage of text, first think about *what might be too difficult*. Is a challenging element impeding progress? For instance, if the student is reading at 89% accuracy, he or she is practicing decoding, not fluency, and the passage would not be appropriate for fluency practice. The student should be reading at 95%+ accuracy for fluency practice.

It is important to assess the student at regular and frequent intervals. The use of manipulatives for segmentation is also helpful in the assessment process. If students are experiencing difficulty, reduce the complexity of the language by limiting the number of syllables or phonemes. Use words that are already familiar to students as part of their natural oral language.

Do not wait to introduce letter–sound relationships, sight vocabulary, and other beginning reading skills until children have mastered phonemic awareness. Initial phoneme recognition and some segmentation ability are all that is required for instruction in beginning phonics—being able to isolate the first sound in a word should be sufficient for instruction in initial consonant correspondences (Lyon, 2000).

Developing Phonological Memory

As noted by Uhry:

Children with dyslexia, or word-level reading disorder, typically memorize individual words, but have difficulty generalizing from one word to another *because of deficits in phonological awareness.*

Verbal, short-term memory is a type of phonological process, as storage involves the use of phonological features. Young readers with difficulty in this type of phonological processing can recode letters to sounds but have *difficulty remembering the sounds long enough to blend them into words.* (Birch, 2002)

Step 1: Phonological Awareness
- Ask students to *listen for sound clues.*
- Have them **hold up one finger for each** *syllable* in the word (or clap their hands once for each syllable).
- Say the word, syllable by syllable, and have students *put down a counter* (colored disc) for each "tiny sound" or phoneme they hear (sounds, not letters).
- You may use nonsense words that contain common spelling units or real words.
- For older students, use science words or other vocabulary from content-area learning.

Step 2: Orthographic Awareness
- Use the same words as in the Step 1 activities.
- Students are to *identify the spelling units* (one- or two-letter clusters) in the words from memory.
- Present the word on a card and ask students to *look carefully* at each letter. Allow 1 second per letter.
- Cover the card or turn it over. Ask students to *close their eyes and form a picture* of the word in their "mind's eye." If working with a small group, have them tell you the spelling units, if a large group, they may write it down.
- Ask the students to *identify the spelling unit in specific positions in the word* and sometimes the whole word. For example, the first and third letter, third and fourth, third and fifth, and so on.
- In *later sessions,* you may provide a word list for each student. Have them *run a finger under the word,* attending to each letter, *cover the word* with a card, then *spell it aloud.*

"Phonemic awareness is most effective when students learn to segment and identify phonemes as part of learning to read and write rather than as an isolated skill. Students *taught by an integrated approach outperform* those who are taught either phonological awareness or phonics in isolation" (Gunning, 2001).

Step 3: Decode the Words
- Have students segment, blend, and identify each spelling unit and rewrite in alternate colors (e.g., red/blue) if they experience difficulty.
- This is followed by instruction in larger units—rimes (discussed in the next section).

Supporting Phonological Skills

Implement the pause–prompt–praise strategy when students come to an unfamiliar word and start to struggle, as follows:

Wait: Pause for at least 10 seconds—students may self-correct.
General Prompt: Encourage self-monitoring and possible identification of a useful strategy with the target word.

Direct student attention to possible sources of information in the text: What can you do to figure it out? Prompt students to take a running start—let them reread and give them a chance to self-monitor and self-correct. You could prompt your students with: "Something puzzled you. Start here (point with pencil to place in text—beginning of phrase or sentence) . . . (or) Show me where that is."

Specific Prompt: Give the student directions. Focus on a word identification strategy and provide context support. For example, you could prompt the student as follows: "Touch and say each sound. Cover up part of the word so you can see the chunk. . . . Find a part you know." As additional support, you could provide a model of what to look for. Write the word on a white board, use magnetic letters, or use the screen spelling technique described in the chapter discussing tactile learners.
Praise and Reinforce: To reinforce the successful strategy and encourage future application, state what they have done. Then have students verbalize what they did. Ask them: "Can you do that next time?

You went back and tried it again . . . broke the word into chunks. It was great the way you used a part of the word that you knew already to help you say the whole word. Tell me how you did that. Let's try it again."

DEVELOPING STRATEGIC STUDENTS

Teaching Strategies: What Do Good Readers Do?

"The kind of work kids actually spend their time doing is a good predictor of what they are likely to learn" (Allington, 1994).

It is important to note that teachers need to change the delivery of instruction, including the output of information and the input required by the student. Think of your typical instructional day. What kind of responses are you asking students to perform? In a study by Allington (1994), he found that many teachers focused on low-level skills instead of higher-level thinking skills that can engage your reluctant readers. When a student's instructional day is spent on low-level tasks such as locating, matching, copying, and listing, there is very little transfer. These tasks do not develop the meaning-making process that is critical for comprehension. Instead, teachers need to utilize higher-level skills that result in greater transfer, such as paraphrasing, explaining, inferring, synthesizing, summarizing, and clarifying.

The implications of this research are quite clear. Teachers need to be more specific and explicit in directly teaching reading strategies so that students can become more engaged and purposeful in the reading process. Students need to be taught to describe the purpose of the reading: Why are we doing this? What did the author have in mind? Teachers can model this through a think-aloud strategy and have students try it out with learning partners.

The importance of teacher modeling of comprehension strategies cannot be overemphasized, especially for struggling readers. Once again, the metacognitive technique of think-alouds should be demonstrated to the students daily by the teacher. This procedure works best when students have a learning partner. Practice and feedback from learning partners provides encouragement during the read-aloud process. Have the students "chunk" the reading material by only reading as much as one hand can cover.

Finally, generalization is a critical reading strategy. Generalization skills can be used across texts and content areas. Ask students to share what they found memorable in the passage with their learning partners. Have them restate ideas in their own words. Perhaps you could have them pretend to be newspapers reporter and generalize the meaning of the passage as a headline.

Ways to Help Students Make Sense of Text

To make sense of text, good readers determine the importance of what they are reading, summarize information, make inferences, generate questions, and monitor their comprehension. The following methods can be used to help students make meaning of what they read throughout the three stages of the reading process.

Before reading. This is a critical phase in the reading process. Students should think about what they already know about the topic. Elicit their ideas verbally or in pictures. Show the book's cover, for example, and have students predict what the text will be about or what will happen next. Record their responses.

While reading. Ask questions continuously throughout teacher read-aloud times. Have the students look for answers to the questions they have. Have them predict what will happen next. Relate what is being read to their background/prior knowledge. Check for meaning by rereading the parts that aren't making sense. Prompt the students to use context clues to determine a new word or meaning of a word. Invite them to retell parts of the text. For the visual learners, ask them to describe the pictures they visualize in their minds. Promote the use of graphic organizers to make sense of text. Have students draw conclusions and inferences based on what is read.

After reading. This is the essential time for your students to recall and reflect on what they have read and to be able to summarize the key points. Students should summarize or retell the important things in the text. Bring the text to life! Have your students dramatize a chunk of the text for the class. Why not transform the story—into another time, with other characters, into another genre, by creating a different ending, and so forth. For the visual learners, have them graphically represent the most important parts, such as by creating a storyboard of the main points of the story or text.

Metacognitive Strategies

In order to get students to think about their thinking, termed *metacognition*, many teachers model the think-aloud strategy as a classroom comprehension technique (Davey, 1983; Nist, S.L., & Kirby, K. (1986). In the think-aloud strategy, the teacher reads aloud from a text and verbalizes thoughts, questions, comments, predictions, reactions, and other responses. This process is to show students what readers do in their minds during the actual reading phase. This promotes reading as an active process of engagement.

Use the following process to implement the think-aloud strategy:

Select a passage for modeling: Select a short passage of 100–300 words to read aloud to students.

Prepare your comments to share: Keep in mind that your purpose is to model your connections to the text as you pause when you read and pose questions to the students.

Explain the technique to students: Tell the students that you are going to share with them "what you think about" as you read.

Read the passage and use "think-aloud" strategies: Share the passage that you selected and stop whenever you have a response. According to Davey (1983), you can include any or all of the following:

- Making predictions
- Visualize the images created
- Sharing comparisons and prior-knowledge connections
- Demonstrating how you would verbalize a confusing point to help clarify it
- Modeling "fix-up" strategies, such as self-correcting or rereading for emphasis or to focus on the meanings of the words

Discuss strategy and answer questions from students: Give students the opportunity to question you about how you think and how you use the think-aloud strategy.

Give students time to practice with learning partners: Have students select a passage to read from their informational text or a chosen story. They are instructed to pre-read the passage, keeping in mind what strategies were modeled for them. They need to pause to reflect on and think about what they read. Encourage them to verbalize their thoughts and processes as they read, taking turns with their partners.

Why should we do this? Wade (1990) states that there are four types of text comprehenders: good comprehenders, non-risk takers, schema imposers, and story-tellers. Wade has found that students may not always share what they are aware of in their reading or be able to verbalize it because they have had limited practice in describing their thinking processes. That is why it is so important to model and practice the think-aloud technique with your students.

Think-Before-You-Read Techniques

In textbooks. Have the students look at pictures and illustrations, maps and charts, captions, chapter titles, section titles, bold words, and the first things and last things in the chapter.

In storybooks. Point out and describe the picture on the cover, read what is on the back cover, and look over the beginning page, any prologue or introduction, and chapter titles.

Students can use a form like the following, in which they finish each sentence, then add one or two more sentences after that.

After I look at the reading, I predict that I will be reading about _____
_____
_____

I already know something about this topic. I know that _____
_____
_____

Something I don't know about this topic and would like to find out more about is
_____
_____
_____

These strategies are great for many students, but what can you do if they can't read the textbook? Try the following:

1. Provide supplemental resources on the topic at a more accessible reading level.
2. Modify the text with one of the following methods:
   - Use graphic organizers and advance organizers to focus their reading.
   - Highlight key portions of the text.
   - Make notes in the margin with sticky notes.
   - Build their background knowledge with interesting supplements, such as Internet images, video clips, pre-teaching interest-building questions, and so forth.
   - Tape record portions of the text or modified versions of the text—students can listen on a MP3 player or iPod.
   - Model and demonstrate the major themes.
   - Read the text as a guided reading group or use shared, interactive, choral, or echo reading.
   - Have students read to learning partners, use the jigsaw method in groups, reciprocal read with partners, or use read-around groups.
   - Review content frequently to assist in sequencing the events for students having difficulty following the storyline.
   - Provide copies of reading material with main ideas underlined or highlighted.
   - Introduce new words by connecting how the words are related to the meaning of the text.
   - Teach students to use an index card or strip to help keep their place on the page and to facilitate tracking.

In conclusion, in reviewing all of the strategies to teach students who learn differently in your inclusive classroom, it is important to always keep in mind the continuum of diverse learners and how we can maximize their success.

Reaching and teaching *all* learners requires extra effort indeed. However, the strategies that are shared in this book require little preparation and are effective in both general education and special education classrooms. They are designed to be successful in all classrooms with students of all ages and ability levels. Differentiation is not a "magic wand"—differentiation is all about dedicating yourself to meet the individual needs of each student who walks through your classroom door!

Let's move forward with more ideas on how to make this happen!

CHAPTER 3

Tactile Strategies
Hands-On Learning

In order for differentiation to be successful, teachers need to integrate instructional strategies that address a broad range of learning styles. This and the following chapters will provide specific techniques that are designed to meet the individual needs of your learners. These strategies should not be confined to inclusive settings and should be considered for all classrooms. The varieties of simple and effective strategies provided address a broad range of learning styles. Each chapter will focus on one predominant learning style to consider in designing differentiated lessons. Here, we start with the tactile learners.

WHO IS THE TACTILE LEARNER?

There are four primary learning styles through which a learner acquires, processes, and retains information: tactile, kinesthetic, visual, and auditory. Tactile learners prefer opportunities where they can actually do something physically with the information they are to learn. Tactile learners learn best through their sense of touch, such as using their hands, fingers, and fine motor skills. Therefore, they learn best by writing, drawing, taking notes, using hands-on manipulatives, and involving their emotions and feelings while learning. The potential advantages of this learning style, if recognized and encouraged by educators and families, can be tremendous.

> Numerous studies in the past three decades have given increased attention to the fact that students learn in diverse ways. As a prominent pedagogical issue, researchers have examined the idea that one approach to teaching does not work for every student (Hawk & Shah, 2007).

Students with a tactile learning style have active hands. They might fiddle with knobs and buttons and examine and evaluate traits of objects. Hands-on learning is the primary method for teaching tactile learners. Tactile learners enjoy the use of manipulatives, building projects, games, making models, and other similar activities.

> Studies have found that students' achievement increases when teaching methods match their learning styles (Dunn, 1990).

WHAT TO LOOK FOR

Hands-on learning is the primary method for teaching tactile learners. Tactile learners manifest a mixture of characteristics while learning new material. The tactile style involves the sense of touch and fine-motor movements as compared to the whole-body movements of the kinesthetic style. Tactile learners take in information through the sense of touch and feeling and they generally have good eye–hand coordination.

These hands-on learners tend to remember information by doing, rather than by listening or seeing. They learn by imitation and practice and love games and group activities. Tactile learners function best with active involvement in learning, such as through model building or project design. Project-oriented methods of learning and science experiments also appeal to these students. On the other hand, some tactile learners tend to struggle with auditory processing and often need things repeated.

Characteristics of Tactile Learners

Characteristics of tactile learners include the following:

- Learn best through hands-on methods, actively exploring the world around them
- Often doodle while listening to help them with processing information
- Tend to find opportunities to fidget with things on the desk
- Rely on what they can directly experience or perform
- Usually talented at drawing designs and constructing things
- Speak with their hands and use gestures to get their ideas across
- Enjoy tasks that involve manipulating materials and objects

WHAT TO DO: STRATEGIES FOR SUCCESS

> When instructional methods are congruent with students' preferred learning style, the greatest achievement gains occur (Masera, 2010).

Many students with special learning needs in your differentiated classrooms are tactile learners. Strategies that utilize a hands-on approach help these students learn and benefit other learners in your classroom as well. Provide things that they can touch that relate to the lesson or topic. They want to move items around with their hands and manipulate articles. The key to addressing a student with a different learning style is to provide a variety of activities and utilize multimodality approaches.

Although many teachers have been taught the value of implementing multimodality instruction in meeting the individual needs of students, there are still classrooms that operate within a traditional "sit-and-get" approach to learning. This method has been found less successful than activity-based and student-centered lessons where students can utilize all of their intelligences and show their knowledge in many different ways.

Tactile learners experience learning by doing the following activities:

- Constructing models
- Performing experiments
- Taking notes
- Preparing multimedia projects
- Drawing, painting, sculpting, and other art-related activities

- Playing games and simulations
- Role-playing
- Making diagrams, mind maps, and word webs
- Collecting stamps, pictures, cards, or other items
- Dancing and related activities

Successful Study Skills

All students, regardless of their learning style, will need to learn compensatory techniques for academic success.

> There has been much empirical evidence supporting the premise that learning styles can hinder or enhance academic performance in many respects. Strategies that support successful study skills in various content areas are of particular importance to student achievement (Riding & Grimley, 1999; Ross & Schultz, 1999).

Tactile learners need to practice concentration and organization techniques in order to achieve their best. Here are some practices that can help tactile learners:

- Making lists of key points
- Holding textbooks rather than lying them flat on a desk
- Reading actively (writing thoughts or questions while reading)
- Note-taking to increase concentration
- Reinforcing the learning of facts using rhythm and movement
- Creating flashcards that can be flipped through for studying
- Using highlighter tape in textbooks
- Sticky notes for marking key ideas in texts and books
- Using a penlight to highlight and follow along in books while reading
- Using a paperclip to move along the edge of book to keep place in text
- Using index cards to keep place in texts
- Using spatial note-taking techniques such as mind-mapping
- Visualizing complex projects from start to finish before beginning using backwards planning, allowing them to keep the big picture in mind
- Skimming and scanning an entire text before reading to get a "feel" about what the text is about, then reading the text carefully

Adaptations for Tactile Learners

There are many simple curriculum modifications and adaptations that you can use in your classroom to better meet the needs of your tactile learners.

> Recent studies concluded that students achieved their highest test scores and expressed a positive attitude toward learning when they were actively engaged with tactile learning techniques (Masera, 2010). It has been found that tactile strategies support all learners by engaging them more in the learning process.

The following is a list of specific tactile strategies that can be implemented in any classroom. These strategies will also benefit other students in the differentiated classroom.

- Tactile game pieces to move on number line to solve math problems
- Rubber pencil grip
- Use of putty or modeling clay

- Pipe cleaners to shape numbers, symbols, and letters
- Fabric "puff paint" to use on paper (creates a raised line that student can trace over)
- Magnetic strips on file cabinets, cookie sheets, or oil drip pans
- Gadget basket filled with small items that students can hold and fiddle with to help them focus
- Wikki Stix (wax-covered string) to form letters or underline key concepts in text
- Question cubes (see further description later in chapter)
- Wet writing on chalkboard using an envelope sealer from a stationary store (the student writes an answer quickly before it evaporates on the board)
- Laminated card stock or file folders that simulate a reusable white board for pupil response
- Zippered plastic bags with small amount of tempera paint for student to finger paint words and math problems

Misconceptions

Instructional materials and approaches in many classrooms remain static and fixed, with a one-size-fits-all mind-set.

> When instruction is not adaptive to meet individual needs, students are expected to cope as best they can. Research suggests that epistemological factors such as lack of attention to information presentation and the perceived difficulties of content are reasons for non-persistence in task completion (Morgan & Tam, 1999; Ozga & Sukhnanden, 1998).

Sometimes tactile learners are misunderstood by parents and teachers because they struggle with traditional forms of assessment and classroom activities. Because of this, they may be labeled as having behavioral or academic problems. A common misconception is that they are performing below grade-level standards and have difficulty processing information. However, tactile learners, because of their energy and social skills, tend to thrive within communities, enjoy team sports, and excel within performing and creative arts. Educators should realize the value of having tactile learners in their classrooms and provide opportunities for them to be successful.

TACTILE TEACHING TOOLS

The following instructional strategies are specifically designed with the needs of tactile learners in mind. Each technique can be modified for different ages and ability levels and different content areas.

Screen Spelling

This is an excellent tactile strategy and a very effective intervention tool for struggling readers. Your first stop is the hardware store. You will need about 4 yards of medium-mesh aluminum screen. It is sold by the yard like fabric. For under $8.00 you can make over 40 screens for your students. Gone are those messy sand trays, cornstarch trays, and tables covered in shaving cream and pudding! Gone are the broken fingernails of cutting out dozens of sandpaper letters!

Spread the screen out on the driveway or sidewalk. With a yardstick and marking pen, make a 9" × 12" grid. Cut out the screens with ordinary kitchen shears—you do not need wire cutters. There will be prickly edges on the screens. They need to be covered with masking tape or duct tape.

To use: have your students place the screen on the table. Place a blank sheet of paper on top of the screen. Students use a crayon to write their spelling or vocabulary words on the papers with the crayon. Primary students can work on letter or number formation. Students then lift off the paper from the screen. Ask them to trace the letters they made with the pointer finger. First they do it with their eyes open and then they trace it with their eyes closed. Next, have them write the word in the air. You will see amazing results!

Index Cards

The use of index cards can be an excellent instructional tool for your tactile learners. Because they are stiffer than ordinary paper, they can be manipulated in many ways to enhance learning. Application suggestions are as follows:

- Students can create their own YES and NO cards (Beninghof, 1998) to use in selected class discussions.
- Students can use index cards to write reports, paragraphs, essays, and poems.
- Index cards may be used for note-taking during a presentation or video
- Colored index cards give students one more way to organize notes or topics for a book report or research project.

Question Card Relay

This is a strategy that involves teamwork, higher-level thinking skills, and the movement of a relay race. Participants work in teams of four. They are each given an envelope with three slips of paper inside. Each student is asked to put a question about the topic being covered on the outside of the envelope and sign it.

At the signal, the teacher will request the students to pass the envelopes to the students to their right. In a finite amount of time (usually 1 or 2 minutes) the recipient looks inside the envelope for a blank card and answers the question to the best of their ability, and then signs the envelope. The teacher gives a signal and another pass occurs. Each student gets a new question, answers it on a blank sheet in the envelope, and signs the envelope. With the next signal, the third and final pass is made and answered. The envelopes are now returned to the "senders." The senders review the responses from their peers to their questions.

The envelopes are then collected by the teacher and reviewed. This is an excellent informal assessment tool, because the teacher gets to know the questions students have and the level of understanding the respondents have.

Puzzle Practice Pairs

Made from index cards cut in two, these puzzles are appealing to both visual and tactile learners. By simply cutting index cards into two pieces that fit together, students can manipulate them to practice and review key concepts in a tactile way that reinforces their learning.

Simple puzzles. A simple set of puzzles may be matched in only one way:

| $3 \times 4 = 12$ | $7 \times 8 = 56$ |

Application suggestions for puzzles include the following:

- Math problems and solutions
- Clock faces and digital times
- States and capitals
- Abbreviations and complete words
- Capital and lowercase letters

Dice Games

You can create a wide variety of highly tactile practice activities for your inclusive classroom by adapting dice. To adapt the cubes, use sticky dots (available where office supplies are sold) or cut mailing labels to fit the faces.

Application suggestions include the following:

- Students may use numbered dice to create addition, subtraction, multiplication, or division problems.
- Alphabet adaptation: Students roll a single die labeled with a different letter on each face. They use the letter that comes up to:
  - ➢ Say the sound(s) the letter makes,
  - ➢ Brainstorm words that begin with the letter, or
  - ➢ Find objects in the room that begin with that letter.
- Color adaptation: Colored labels are attached to dice, and students name the color they roll.
- Geography adaptation: Dice are labeled with the names of states, countries, capitals, continents, oceans, or other geographic features. Students point to these on a map as they are rolled.

"Wikki Stix"

Wikki Stix are lengths of wax-covered yarn available in toy stores and educational supply stores. Because of their sticky texture, they adhere to paper and can be reused over and over again.

Application suggestions include the following:

- Forming shapes, letters, numbers, names, and words
- Underlining or circling key points, topic sentences, or important dates and names in a text
- Underlining directions on a worksheet
- Forming margins on a piece of writing paper
- Serving as an alternative to pencils for matching activities

Magnetic Strips, Letters, and Shapes

By backing any sturdy paper with a length of magnetic strip, teachers can easily construct magnetic practice activities at varying levels of sophistication.

Application suggestions include the following:

- Matching
  - ➢ Vocabulary and definitions
  - ➢ Coins and monetary values

➤ Math equations
➤ People and accomplishments
• Sequencing
➤ Historical timelines
➤ Events in a story plot
➤ Steps in a process

Sponge Writing

Using envelope sealers (commonly available at office supply stores) or pieces of sponge cut into manageable cubes and dampened with water, students write on individual chalkboards or at the classroom chalkboard. Sponge writing may be used to encourage writing fluency and reinforces tactile learners by providing an additional stimulus. If a chalkboard is not accessible, a similar effect can be created by applying the moistened sponge tip to a sheet of construction paper, which will absorb the letters or numbers written.

Application suggestions include the following:

• Letter or number formation
• Spelling words
• Math facts or more complex computations
• Handwriting practice (without an emphasis on speed)

Reinforcing with Puffy Craft Paint

Traditional paper used in the classroom has a flat surface that provides little reinforcement for the tactile learners. The use of puffy craft paint (available at hobby and craft stores), with its 3-D texture, provides students with a slightly raised surface on the paper that they can trace with their fingers to reinforce concepts (Beninghof, 1998).

Application suggestions include the following:

• Reinforce the margins on students' writing paper by providing a raised line as a guide.
• Box or mark directions on worksheets or within workbooks.
• Add dots of craft paint to critical aspects of a number chart or number line for tactile emphasis.
• Create tactile worksheets for students.

Finger-Paint Zip-Top Bags

Fill a good-quality strong zip-top bag with a small amount of tempera or finger paint. Place the open bag on a flat surface and carefully smooth it out toward the opening to release trapped air. Seal the bag tightly. Reinforce the edges with layers of clear tape. You have just created a finger-paint bag (Beninghof, 1998)—a simple way to combine tactile and visual input for your students.

Students can "write" on the surface of the paint bags using their fingertips or a pencil-tip eraser. The bag can be "erased" by smoothing its surface with the hand. The student can then create a new word for reinforcement and practice.

Application suggestions include the following:

- Forming letters or numbers
- Practicing spelling words

Flip Books

Flip books are engaging and provide tactile learners with a hands-on strategy that they can use independently or with learning partners. Flip books are easily made out of a standard size sheet of paper or 9" × 12" sheets of construction paper. Students fold the paper in half lengthwise, and then fold it in fourths. They then cut on the fold to the mid-point crease to create four flaps.

They are multiple uses for flip books. The outside flaps could be math problems, and the inside flaps would show the solutions. Vocabulary words and definitions could also be used. Students could draw the main characters of a story on the outside flaps and write descriptions of the characters on the inside.

"Cootie Catcher" Quiz Picks

The timeless childhood pastime of creating "cootie catchers" (Beninghof, 1998) is a wonderful, game-like device for practicing/reviewing any type of short-answer content. They may be transformed into learning tools by labeling the four exterior surfaces with numbers or color words, and the next inner layer with questions or problems. Beneath each question or problem is its answer.

Application suggestions:

- Geography facts
- Reading vocabulary and definitions
- Addition, subtraction, multiplication, and division facts
- Important historical dates or facts

Peek-Through Page Protectors

Page protectors are clear, acetate report covers that may be placed over pages in a textbook. With these "magic covers" in place, a student is able to make marks or write just as though he or she were writing directly on the text page.

Application suggestions include the following:

Teacher use:
- Highlight directions.
- Select certain problems or questions for student attention.
- Change subtraction signs to addition signs.
- Divide the page into manageable sections.

Student use:
- Complete computations on the page.
- Circle designated letters or words.
- Underline or circle challenging words or sentences.
- Mark new information or respond to the text.

"Bean Boggle"

This is a great tactile word-building technique that all of your students will enjoy. Stop by your grocery store and get a 2-pound bag of flat white lima beans in the dried bean aisle. You will need two permanent fine-tip markers—one in red (for vowel sounds) and one in black (for consonant sounds). You will also need a box of "snack-size" zip-top bags to place the "alpha beans" in when finished. Use the black marker to print consonant letters on the beans. With the red pen, print vowel sounds on other beans. Leave some beans blank. These are "wild card" beans and can be used for any letter that the student needs.

Place an assortment of letter beans in each bag. This can be differentiated by using it as an independent activity for word building with the beans in a Scrabble-style game. It can also be used for word building in partners or teams. Make multiple beans of vowel sounds and multiples of the most frequently used consonants.

This strategy not only utilizes the tactile strengths of your students, but also involves eye–hand coordination and fine motor skills.

Cubing

Cubing is a strategy designed to help students think about a topic or idea from many different angles. Tactile students like this hands-on approach. It is an excellent way to differentiate the process and the product of the topic that you are working on. Cubes can be used to differentiate activities on the basis of student readiness.

A cube includes six commands—one on each of its six faces—followed by a prompt that describes the task the student should do related to the command. For example:

Command: DESCRIBE
Prompt: Describe photosynthesis using as much information as you can, and involving as many senses as possible in your description.

Command: EVALUATE
Prompt: Evaluate the importance of photosynthesis and its relationship to global warming.

Cubing is a motivating way to differentiate curriculum using choice and chance and allows the student to have at least six variations of a task to complete related to the content of the lesson. Further differentiation can occur if teachers color-code the cubes to correspond to various readiness levels, student interest, or the learning styles of individual students.

Each face of the cube can have one of the following open-ended prompts so that the cube can be used for multiple lessons:

- Who?
- What?
- Where?
- Why?
- When?
- How?

For younger students, each of these questions can be placed on a cube that is easily made out of a small child-sized milk carton that has had the top removed and all sides covered with construction paper

Another application is to have students read a story with their learning partners and then take turns rolling the cube. Depending on what question lands on top, the student answers the question based on the facts of the story. Then the other student gets to roll.

Other open-ended prompts include the following:

- Connect
- Analyze
- Compare
- Explain
- Diagram
- Synthesize

An accompanying worksheet can be prepared in advance to give the students more details about the expected outcomes. You can also use dice to create the same effect: In advance, create a worksheet that lists each number on the dice (1–6) and a corresponding task relating to the lesson. The students roll the dice and complete the task for the number rolled.

Question Cubes

Question cubes were developed by Elizabeth Cowan-Neeld (1980). They create a game-like atmosphere and will increase the attentiveness and involvement of all your students, especially your tactile and visual learners.

Make a question cube using the following steps (see Figure 3.1):

1. Use two small milk cartons (the size usually sold by the school lunch program) to create the cube. Cut the tops off both cartons and insert one, bottom side up, into the other, creating a closed cube.
2. Cover the cube with plain sticky-backed paper.
3. On each face, write a question word: What? When? Where? Who? Why? How?

Other application suggestions include the following:

- Have students generate questions about whatever content is being studied.
- Teach students how to formulate comprehension questions at varying levels of complexity.
- Have students work with partners as they read a content-rich selection.

Figure 3.1. Cubing Pattern

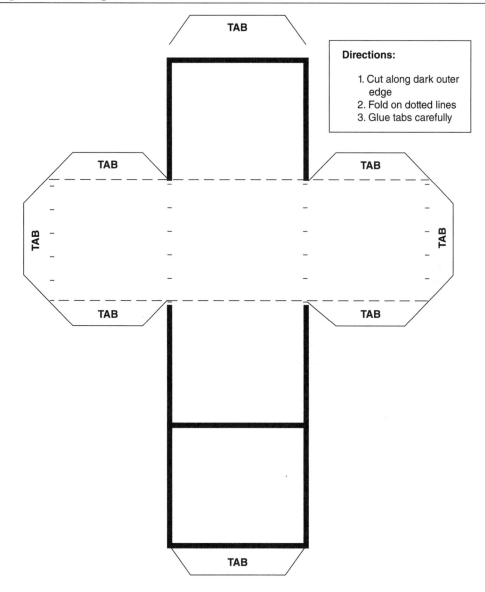

Directions:

1. Cut along dark outer edge
2. Fold on dotted lines
3. Glue tabs carefully

IDEAS FOR PROFESSIONAL DEVELOPMENT LEADERS

Ask participants what they know about learning styles and differentiation techniques. What impact has this had on their teaching?

Discuss what the instructional advantages are of being aware of differing learning styles in inclusive classrooms. Have them share their thoughts. Have they experienced any challenges in integrating strategies for different learning styles into their teaching and curriculum? Provide examples.

SEMANTIC SORT

Overview

The semantic sort strategy is an excellent way to build higher-level thinking skills with students. It is a word sort strategy in which the students are asked to categorize key vocabulary into groups that make sense to them. In so doing, they discuss their thinking processes with learning partners concerning the words, their meanings, and how they are connected to the other words. It is an easy-to-use strategy because the teacher only needs to identify and duplicate key vocabulary words of the selection to be read. This strategy can work effectively to boost comprehension with both narrative and/or expository text. Tactile learners enjoy being able to manipulate and sort the words as they discuss their meaning.

Implementation

1. Select 10 to 20 key words (depending on the length of the reading passage).
2. Type up each word on a sheet of paper and copy enough for partner work. Students will then cut the words apart into separate "word chips" to manipulate and sort.
3. Before reading the passage, ask students to sort the words in a way that makes the most sense to them. Ask them to predict what they think is going to happen. You'll undoubtedly receive a variety of responses.
4. During the reading, stop at a key point or halfway through the passage. Give students the opportunity to re-sort their words with their partner. Ask them to share how and why they chose to re-sort or not re-sort. Partners may share ideas with others.
5. After reading, have partners complete a final sort of their words. This time they need to record their sort, and both partners need to write their interpretations of the sort into their Word Study notebooks or on lined paper. This may be assigned for homework.
6. Have students share and discuss their interpretations of the sorts the next day (or another day), but not that same day.

This activity allows students to recognize words in context and to continually refine what they understand from the passage by reading, rereading, and rechecking for meaning.

Review the tactile strategies described in this chapter. Have participants form small groups and discuss how these strategies might be adapted for their inclusive classrooms.

Make sample products of tactile tools that have been described in this chapter. Pass them out to the group members so that they can see and manipulate them.

Brainstorm with the group application ideas for each strategy. Some prompts include the following:

*   Specifically, how would you use this technique with your students?
*   What subject area(s) would be most conducive for this strategy?
*   What variations might be helpful for the ages and ability levels of your students?

CHAPTER 4

Auditory Strategies
Tuning in to Literacy

WHO IS THE AUDITORY LEARNER?

> Auditory learners tend to thrive in classrooms where listening and talking are encouraged. They need to hear to understand, and they learn best by listening to content explained. They tend to have difficulty with instructions that are written because they find it hard to make pictures or visualize concepts in their minds (Kostelnik, Soderman, & Whiten, 2004).

Auditory learners tend to go by sound rather than another mode. They have excellent memory for things they have heard, are very verbal, and tend to excel at word games. If they can hear it, they can usually remember it. Because the auditory learner uses this sensory channel to learn best, teachers should tune in to techniques that strengthen this mode. Auditory learners use this method of retention to best grasp the ideas they are given. Traditional classroom teaching is geared toward auditory and visual learners, so auditory learners, which make up about 30% of the population, have an advantage.

Because auditory learners learn best by hearing information, they need opportunities to practice saying words and their definitions so that they can remember them. They also benefit from practicing key concepts by saying them out loud. Auditory learners learn best by hearing information a first time, then hearing themselves or another person say it again. In school, the auditory learner tends to listen to a statement and then repeat it to the teacher for reinforcement. Similarly, when memorizing a phone number, an auditory learner will say it out loud and then remember how it sounded when spoken to recall it.

WHAT TO LOOK FOR

Many auditory learners are the students in the classroom who are whistling while doing their work, or the ones who need to subvocalize while reading "silently," or sing to remember the facts. By listening to their speech patterns, you will notice how auditory students think (e.g., phrases such as the following: that sounds right; I hear you; that really rings a bell; that clicks with me). What seems to be disruptive behavior characterized by their vocalizations is actually helping these students learn. Auditory learners are most likely to enjoy performances where lines are spoken, and they tend to be very good in collaborative groups or teams. They are likely to be interested in the volume, tone, and harmony of what they hear, and thus music has a special impact for them.

Because auditory learners tend to thrive in class discussions, they often depend on telling stories and solve problems by talking about them. Because they are the most talkative students, they can also be easily distracted.

Here are some other characteristics to look for in the classroom:

- They tend to be natural listeners and remember what they hear.
- They may speak slowly and say words in syllables.
- They are easily distracted by noises.
- They may talk while they write or read and tend to read at a slower pace.
- They may seem to be listening to something else rather than the person they are communicating with.
- They prefer to have things explained to them rather than written down.
- They remember by verbalizing and listening.
- They follow spoken directions well.
- They may have difficulty being quiet for extended periods of time.
- They may have trouble spelling in written work but can spell well verbally.
- The often enjoy the performing arts.
- They tend to be natural listeners.
- They are not afraid to speak in class.
- They may have trouble remembering what is read if it was not vocalized.
- They have strong language skills, an appreciation for words, and a broad vocabulary.
- They are good at explaining things to others and like giving oral reports.
- They can articulate their ideas clearly and have strong oral communication skills.
- They may have difficulty interpreting complex visuals such as graphs, maps, and charts.
- They often have musical talents and enjoy listening to music.

WHAT TO DO: STRATEGIES FOR SUCCESS

What we hope to do in education is to strengthen the skills of students across the entire spectrum of learning styles so that they learn to use more than one intelligence and thus can fully benefit from comprehensive instruction. For auditory learners, teachers should provide as much verbal stimuli as possible through verbal interactions and reinforcement, class discussions, and activities with learning partner. Repetitive drills, rhythmic rhymes and "raps," and teacher and student read-alouds are also helpful techniques.

Here are some strategies that have worked well with the auditory learners in my classes:

- Have books on CD, especially if such students are reading independently. Offer this option whenever possible.
- Choral read directions or have students repeat or explain the directions.

- Have students record facts set to music.
- Read aloud any written information—such as text, stories, and directions.
- Help students use word associations to remember facts and concepts.
- Have students repeat facts with their eyes closed.
- Instead of having students take tests in writing, have them tape record their responses.
- Use videos to enhance learning.
- Provide opportunities for group (or partner) activities and discussions.
- Use the "Triple Talk" (Beninghof, 1995) technique by repeating an important phrase three times to boost students' retention of the concept. A similar technique is the use of "chanting," where the students respond to a key phrase by chanting it out loud together. This also helps to promote fluency.
- Have students call their homes from school to leave messages regarding school on their own answering machines (e.g., homework, required signatures, success stories).
- Have students tape record lesson notes after writing them.
- Use interactive computer programs.
- Have students explain what they have learned to study partners.
- Provide adequate time for discussions or allow the students to create study groups.
- Allow time for students to retell a story or the key concepts of a chapter in their own words.
- Give assignments in small chunks so they do not overwhelm students.
- Use noisemakers to gain attention and use different sounds for different types of directions.
- Use a variety of vocal tones to indicate transitions between activities in the classroom.
- Teach students to use mnemonic devices to help them remember concepts and facts.
- Tape record individual students reading and have them listen to the recordings for reinforcement.
- Have silencer headphones available that students can use to block out extraneous background noise.
- Avoid oververbalizing (e.g., keep directions simple, be succinct) and lecture actively, pausing frequently for greater retention.
- Use the "ask three before me" strategy—before asking the teacher for help, students are to first ask three peers for assistance.
- Put information into a rhythmic pattern such as a rap, poem, or song (Kostelnik et al., 2004) to help capture student attention and promote retention.

In addition, have your auditory learners:

- Participate in group (or partner) activities.
- Answer comprehension questions orally.
- Read along with books on CD or mp3 players.
- Talk aloud while reading instructions for a literature assignment.

- Read aloud to themselves (or partners).
- Verbally repeat key points.
- Drill math facts out loud with partners.
- Use narrative reporting instead of traditional written book reports.
- Give oral presentations instead of written essays.
- Set information to familiar tunes and sing it.
- Make tapes of class notes and then listen to them.
- Whisper new information when alone (Vincent & Ross, 2001).
- Remember details by trying to "hear" previous discussions in their minds.

Students with auditory preferences might also benefit from the following:

Dialogues	Radio interviews	iPod use
Learning partners	Peer tutoring	Oral summaries
Debates	Monologues	Cross-age tutoring
Role-plays	Recorded books	Stories in Power Point
Interviews	Podcasts	format with narrative
CD recordings	Dramatic skits	Interactive websites
Video clips	Impersonations of	Musical narratives
Humming, whistling	characters	Recorded texts and
sounds	Oral quizzes	stories
Panel discussion	Concentration games	Questioning the teacher
Teaching the class	Oral surveys of classmates	Poetry readings
Storytelling	Jeopardy-type games	
Puppet shows	Reading aloud	

SUCCESSFUL STUDY SKILLS

Because auditory learners learn best while they are actively listening, traditional study practices, such as note-taking from the text, may not be effective. The following tips for teachers can help auditory learners in the classroom:

Present information verbally. Any new lesson information or key points should be stated aloud so that questions can be verbalized and internalized by students needing auditory stimuli. Just reading alone or seeing the information visually will not help as much as hearing important material. To learn a sequence of steps, saying it aloud is best for these learners. They should also reason through solutions out loud.

Pair up students with partners or groups. Pair up auditory learners or create study groups so that students will be able to say the material aloud or read it to each other for greater retention. Auditory learners will feel more confident with personal understanding.

Allow time for questions. Allow time for your auditory learners to ask questions during a lesson. This will help them clarify points they may otherwise miss. In addition, periodically question students or ask them to paraphrase key concepts, which greatly increase retention. Allowing time for students to ask questions and asking questions of the students will ensure greater student engagement by involving them in the lesson, and give you the opportunity to check for understanding.

The following tips for students will also help the auditory learners in your classroom:

Make up unusual or crazy songs. Encourage auditory learners to make up songs to go along with their study materials, which will provide the sound stimulus that they require. The more unusual the song or rap and the more it is connected to the material to be learned, the better the information will be retained.

Tape lesson notes. An excellent tip for auditory learners is to tape record themselves reading their written lecture notes aloud. In addition, you could encourage the tape recording of other instructional materials in the classroom. Recording lessons of any kind will ensure that everything important is in auditory form that can be accessed at the student's leisure.

Use word association. Auditory learners should be encouraged to review their notes and make appropriate word associations with concepts learned to increase memory of key facts. Provide modeling to get students started.

Recommend the use of mnemonics. Another form of word association and an excellent tool to aid memory is the use of mnemonics, such as rhymes or word patterns that can be said aloud to foster instant recall. Encourage students to make up their own nonsense rhymes. This will help them with creating greater meaning and memory.

Avoid auditory distractions. Auditory learners are easily distracted by extraneous noise. A bit of quiet music or the use of headphones may increase retention and attention to the assignment or materials.

A CLOSER LOOK: STRATEGIES FOR SUCCESS FOR AUDITORY LEARNERS

Reading Trios

The reading trios strategy, in which groups of three read material together, was developed by Ed Gickling (Gickling & Rosenfield, 1995). The three roles are as follows:

Reader: One student reads a paragraph aloud.
Reteller: One student listens in order to retell as much of the information as possible.
Checker: One student listens in order to monitor the accuracy of the reteller.

Put Your Two-"Sense" Worth In

This is an adaptation of Linda Hoyt's "Two-Word Strategy" (Hoyt, 1999). The purpose is for students to synthesize information from a story or lesson verbally. After reading, have students write only two words that reflect their thinking about the material. They then share their two words with partners, explaining why they chose them and how they relate to the story and/or their personal lives. Then, they listen to the "two-sense worth" from their partners. After partner sharing, create a class list of all the words using an "alphabox" grid, and the students will then have a word bank for that story or chapter. An "alphabox" grid can easily be developed by placing the letters of the alphabet in individual boxes on a grid. This serves as a vocabulary word bank for the students.

I Remember This . . .

Students work with learning partners in this strategy. Each student takes turns reading a small section of the text or story. For primary students, this can be done as a teacher read-aloud or you can ask them to read "only as much as your hand can cover." This helps to chunk the information and is a powerful support for struggling readers. After silently reading the material, the students cover the page or the text that they read with one hand. They are asked to remember a key idea from the reading and share it with their partners, describing what they found memorable (adapted from Hoyt, 1999).

If using expository text, the following are guiding questions:

- What is the topic?
- What are the most important ideas to remember?
- What is the setting for this information?
- What did you notice about the organization and text structure?
- What did you notice about the visuals—graphs, charts, and pictures?
- Can you remember what you learned?
- What do you think was the author's purpose for writing this text?

"Foggiest Point"

At the end of a lesson or story or after reading a chapter in a text, have students share with partners their "foggiest point"—that is, material that they need greater clarity on. You can also ask the students to put these points in writing and collect them to assess student understanding. The valuable part for auditory learners is the sharing and listening with their partners.

"Read to the Beat"

When you do a teacher read-aloud, find music that complements the words and the message and play it softly in the background. You can ask students to finger snap or chime in with a melodic refrain or repeat certain segments. This musical background can really enhance the message of the story you are sharing for auditory learners.

Outcome Sentences

Outcome sentences can be used with any grade level and any content area. It is a strategy where students reflect on what they learn either in writing or verbally. See the example in Figure 4.1. If they do it in writing, they can share it with partners, and this reinforces the learning for auditory students. They can also submit their responses when leaving the classroom as **"exit tickets"**—the teacher stands at the door and students must turn in their exit cards before they leave. This is an excellent informal assessment method for the teacher to gather information about students' key understandings and to guide lesson planning for the next day.

"Idea Wave"

At the end of a lesson, use this verbal recall technique as a fast reflection on key ideas. Start the "wave" at one side of the classroom. Display open-ended prompts so that students can respond verbally to the content and key points of the lesson or story. The "wave" continues throughout the room. Each student in turn provides a verbal response to the prompt of their choice. Students have to listen carefully so they do not repeat another's response. You can use the prompts for the outcome sentences shown in Figure 4.1.

Vocabulary Relay

This is an active strategy that requires active listening and verbal responses. This strategy is sometimes called "I have . . . Who has?" Auditory learners excel at this engaging structure that is used to review vocabulary words and their definitions. The process is as follows:

- Have students write one definition only on an index card (the word itself should not be included).
- The cards are then turned in to the teacher.

Figure 4.1. Outcome Statements

Take a few minutes to reflect upon today's class session.
Think back over our activities, presentations, and discussions.
See if you can find some important learnings and discoveries for yourself.
Write your thoughts beginning with these phrases:

I learned . . . _____

_____

I discovered . . . _____

_____

I observed . . . _____

_____

I was surprised . . . _____

_____

I am beginning to wonder . . . _____

_____

I now realize . . . _____

_____

I would like to find out more about . . . _____

_____

I am still confused about . . . _____

_____

_____

- The teacher takes the cards and writes one vocabulary word on the back of each card, making sure that the word does NOT match the definition. (It helps to put the words on sticky-notes first to make sure that no two cards directly cancel each other out.)
- Next, hand the cards out so that each student has one card. If there are more cards than students, you may give more than one card to each student. If there are fewer cards than students, then repeat the following process as often as needed to make sure that everyone has had a turn.
- Begin by reading a definition; the student who has that word on his or her index card should stand and say the word, for example, "I have _____." If they are correct, then they should read the definition on the other side of the card: "Who has (definition on the other side of the card)?" If they are incorrect, they wait until the correct answer is read.
- This can be used as a competition among classes or teams within the same classroom.
- An adaptation for primary students is to use common sight words or pictures. An example of the use of sight words might be as follows: (First student) "I have *me*. Who has *like*?" (Second student) "I have *like*. Who has *put*?" (Third student) "I have *put*. Who has *other*?"

Backtracking

For auditory learners, backtracking is a wonderful predictive strategy that heightens their listening and prediction skills.

First, you (the teacher) read the only a few of the *end* pages of a book. Do not give any "text tours" or preview of the pictures. After they have heard the end of the story, ask students, "What do you think this story will be about? Why?" Record responses, and then read the book in a traditional manner and compare predictions with the book's actual events.

QUESTION FAN

Overview

The question fan strategy uses open-ended response stems from varying levels of Bloom's taxonomy of higher-level thinking skills. It can be used by the teacher after a read-aloud to have students respond more creatively and to have them more closely analyze their responses to the story. Divergent thinking is promoted rather than just literal retelling of the facts.

Students can use this strategy with learning partners in a reciprocal teaching situation or between pairs.

Implementation

Use the following steps to implement the strategy:

- Duplicate the list of questions on different colors of card stock to represent the different levels of Bloom's taxonomy.

- Cut the card stock into question strips.
- Arrange the strips in a stack in a hierarchical order from:
  - ➤ Knowledge level
    - When and where does this story take place?
    - What is the problem in the story?
    - How does the story end?
  - ➤ Comprehension level
    - Explain why the story has the title it does.
    - How did the main character feel at the beginning of the story? At the end?
    - How was the problem in the story solved?
  - ➤ Analysis level
    - What do you do that is similar to or different from what the person in the story did?
    - What things in the story could really happen?
    - What part of the story was the funniest? Or the saddest? Or the most exciting?
  - ➤ Application level
    - If you had to cook a meal for the main character, what would you cook and why?
    - What would your mother or another member of your family do if she or her were in the story?
    - What would you do if you could go where the story takes place?
  - ➤ Synthesis level
    - Think of two or three new titles for the story.
    - Retell the story from another character's point of view.
    - How else could the story end?
  - ➤ Evaluation level
    - Compare two of the characters.
    - Would you recommend this book to a friend? Why or why not?
    - Was the main character in the story good or bad? Explain your answer.
- Hole-punch the ends of the question strips and connect them with a brass paper brad.
- Now fan them out and you have multiple questions at many levels to ask your learners about ANY story.
- You can differentiate instruction with the question fan by assigning students of different readiness levels to different colors of questions.

READER'S THEATRE: A PURPOSE FOR REREADING

"Ample rehearsal time makes the difference for struggling readers. There should be a regular sequence of activities leading to the performance. The sequence should include choosing texts (teacher and students jointly), practicing in small groups and at home, and teacher feedback and support during small group practice" (Worthy & Broaddus, 2001).

Overview

Reader's Theatre is performance reading without the costumes and props, movement, or memorization of lines. Students practice in a group and individually before reading for an audience. Different groups may perform for another group or for the whole class. Because Reader's Theatre does not involve acting, props, costumes, or scenery, readers use their voices to bring forth the meaning. This is a boost for auditory learners and promotes fluency.

Research has supported the power of Reader's Theatre to improve fluency, listening comprehension, and reading performance. The process supports student engagement and motivation as well (Kuhn & Stahl, 2003; Rasinski, 2004).

Implementation

Follow these easy steps for starting Reader's Theatre:

- *Involve* students in turning a favorite piece into a script in a shared writing format.
- *Delete* unneeded parts and *add* lines that will contribute to the script.
- *Choose* scripts that are fun to do and that are rich in dialogue and action.
- Lines not in dialogue form can be given to narrators—Reader 1, Reader 2, and so forth.
- Start *slowly* and allow students to feel comfortable in the performance mode.
- *Staging* is not necessary; work in small groups when possible.
- *Pre-teach* new vocabulary and concepts for clear understanding.

In addition, the following are helpful tips for using Reader's Theatre in the classroom:

- Students may all practice the same script, or give different scripts to "repertory groups" to learn for the week. Provide a copy of the script for each child, with an additional one for home use.
- Read the script slowly to students several times. Ensure students' eyes are on the script following along as you read.
- Echo read the script with the whole class or groups.
- Begin with very easy scripts at first.
- Select scripts that involve many readers and many students working together.
- Assign roles. You may have several students in the same role:
  - ➤ Mark roles with a highlighter.
  - ➤ Students with the same role can work together.
- Readers soon learn that it is the *expression* in their voices that adds drama to the story.
- Provide multiple practice opportunities to read the script as a class, in groups, and independently.
- Students may take their scripts home for additional practice.
- When students are ready, perform for an audience, such as the class next door, the office staff, or a kindergarten class.

TEXT TALK AND WALK

Overview

This is a powerful group prereading strategy, particularly suited to auditory as well as kinesthetic learners. It involves oral language fluency and interaction. This strategy is adapted from cooperative learning structures developed by Kagan, (2000).

Implementation

Use the following steps to implement the "text talk and walk" strategy in the classroom:

- Select a number of sentences or phrases from the text or story to be read. Make enough strips for these sentences or phrases so that everyone in the class has one (they may be repeated to reinforce the learning). Select quotes or phrases that are significant to the text. They should reveal enough about the story or the chapter so that the students think along the lines that support text understanding.
- Pass out the "text talk" strips. Students read their strips to themselves and rehearse them (important for struggling readers), reflecting on what impressions they now have about the text or story based on this information.
- Small-group version: Students take turns sharing their strips and listening to others with no discussion. After all the strips have been read, each student writes a final impression that they now have about the text. Some things they may want to consider are the following:
  - ➣ What is it about?
  - ➣ What do we know about the characters?
  - ➣ What do we think will happen?
  - ➣ What will we learn about the topic?

They will discuss their ideas with the group. After that, certain speakers from each group may share their ideas with the rest of the class. After reading the story or text, remind the students of this activity and their responses. Discuss the similarities and differences in the pre-discussion and the actual story events.

- Whole-class version: *mix-mingle-music*
  - ➣ All students receive one strip. They rehearse and read their strips to themselves.
  - ➣ When music starts, they begin to roam around the room, sharing their "text tidbit" with as many students as possible before the song is over. Sharing proceeds as follows: "Did you know that _____?" and then listening to another student's text tidbit.
  - ➣ When the music stops, they return to their seats and verbally share what they found out with their learning partners.
  - ➣ The learning pair then makes a prediction about what the story or text will be like.

Adapted from Kagan, 1994

"PHANTASTIC PHONICS PHONE"

Overview

The phonics phone is a simple tube shaped like a telephone receiver, made from plastic PVC pipe (two "elbows" and a "coupling"). These hollow tubes allow a student to speak quietly into one end and hear his or her own voice from the other. Students use the phone to listen to their own voice as they practice reading.

How Do They Enhance Reading Instruction?

Because the pipe funnels the student's voice directly into the ear, this helps the students acquire phonemic awareness. The phone compels the student to whisper because it amplifies the sound. The phone also improves student focus and attention because they are intentionally listening to their own voice. This allows the entire classroom to quietly read orally without disturbing each other. The phones provide a level of privacy that is particularly important to struggling adolescent readers.

Implementation

The phones can also be used to help students develop necessary higher-level skills in vocabulary, fluency, and comprehension. Older students can use the phones to edit their essays. They read aloud to catch mistakes and then make the necessary revisions. Auditory learners thrive with the use of this device.

In independent reading, the phones are beneficial in:

- Improving self-correction
- Developing fluency
- Practicing expression
- Advancing intermediate-level students
- Providing "privacy" for older struggling readers

Consider using the phonics phone with the following activities:

- Speech development activities
- Spelling practice
- Editing and proofreading of papers
- Helping English learners
- Practicing for a play, presentation, or speech

Instructions for making phonics phones: PVC pipes come in various sizes and widths. For phonics phones, teachers usually select diameters of 1½ to 2 inches. Make sure that the elbow pieces have the same diameter. You fit them together and use PVC glue to hold them in place. Price varies, but they can be made for well under $2.00 each. They are also available commercially at a greater cost.

Keeping the phones clean is a simple process. Each student can have his or her own phone and store it in a zip-top bag. You can also use antiseptic wipes to cleanse the phones before each use.

Enjoy reading with your students using the phonics phones!

CHAPTER 5

Visual Strategies
The Eyes Have It for Reading

WHO IS THE VISUAL LEARNER?

Visual learners learn best by seeing information. There are two pathways for visual learners—*linguistic* and *spatial*. Students who are visual-linguistic learners tend to learn through written language. If something is written down, they remember it better. They can remember lessons better if they watch them. They like to write down directions before completing a task.

Students with a visual-spatial learning style think in pictures rather than words and tend to have some difficulty with written language. For this reason, children with a visual-spatial learning style may have difficulty learning to read in a traditional auditory-sequential classroom.

In some classes, the visual-spatial learning style is not adequately addressed. Traditional instructional techniques, with their dependence on drill and repetition, step-by-step sequencing, and lectures, favor auditory learners (Silverman, 1989). Teachers who integrate pictures, clip art, and graphics into phonics and reading curriculum materials are much more successful in teaching visual-spatial learners to decode and comprehend. Once visual learners create a mental image of the concepts to be learned and connect it with what they already know, the learning becomes more permanent.

Visual thinking is vital to comprehension. Students need opportunities to explore the impact of visual input on supporting writing and communication (Coleman, Bradley, & Donovan, 2012).

WHAT TO LOOK FOR

The following characteristics are typical of visual learners, who make up the majority of the population (about 65%) and absorb and take in information best by seeing (Felder & Silverman, 1988) due to their strong visual processing skills:

- Information presented in pictures, charts, or diagrams is easily remembered.
- Tend to be organized and tidy in their workspaces and study areas.

- Need to see the teacher's facial expressions and body language for understanding.
- Can make "movies in their minds" of information they are reading.
- Tend to have the "big-picture" view, especially when studying the parts or details of a topic.
- Visual-spatial skills, such as those relating to size, shape, texture, angles, and 3-D depth, are strong.
- They often pay close attention to the body language of others.
- Outside noises or music often distracts their ability to focus and pay attention to a task.
- They enjoy learning through visually appealing materials.
- They may appear to "tune out" during lengthy lectures.
- They have an instinctive sense of balance, order, and completeness.
- They usually establish eye contact when speaking.
- Retention is improved if they are first allowed to read a passage silently before partner or group work.
- They will take notes during lectures, even if provided with an advance organizer, so that they can refer to the notes later.
- They tend to have great attention to details.
- They think of visual cues and associations to help them remember information.
- They may develop three-dimensional models when studying a new concept.
- They benefit from previewing reading materials.
- They have a keen awareness of aesthetics—the beauty of the physical environment, visual media, or art.
- They prosper when shown or allowed to create graphs and graphic organizers such as webs, concept maps, and idea maps.
- They have a great instinctive sense of direction.
- Prefer a quiet place to study.
- They can easily visualize objects, pictures, and colors.
- They love drawing, scribbling, and doodling.
- They would rather watch than talk or do.
- They benefit from making their own notes, even from written information.
- The may have trouble following verbal directions or attending to long lectures.
- They often look to see what others are doing and copy the behavior.

WHAT TO DO: STRATEGIES FOR SUCCESS

Many teaching strategies can maximize the learning environment for visual learners. Any activity that allows students to form visual images in their minds of what they are learning will not only assist the visual learners, but will enhance the learning of all students. A visual learner's educational experience can be reinforced when new information, concepts, or ideas are presented in a way that supports the visual learning style.

Strategies to assist visual learners include the following:

- Before a lecture, provide students with major points to be covered.
- Include at least one or two visual learning aids in each lecture, such as a chart, graph, or video clip.
- Supplement verbal instructions with additional handouts or diagrams, or write the steps on the board.
- Provide demonstrations that show learners how to complete a required task or assignment.
- Put key words on cards and have students arrange them into sentences.
- Have student make mind maps or concept maps to help organize the material learned and show the connections between the information.
- Use the every-pupil-response technique of individual white boards to have the learners show what they know.
- Seat your visual learners in the front of the classroom for greater access to the board and to reduce distractions.
- Use a sight-word approach to spelling and word study rather than limiting instruction to phonics.
- Encourage retention by relating material to what has already been covered and what will be covered next, and then relating this to the personal experiences of students.
- Incorporate colorful and tangible learning activities that include the use of flashcards, puzzles, posters, and similar items. Have students make their own flashcards to retain important information.
- Use computer-assisted instruction to reinforce key concepts.
- Encourage visual learners to summarize key facts in a graphic organizer as a symbolic summary.
- Provide supplemental charts, graphs, videos, color-coded notes, and flashcards to enhance the learning retention of visual learners.
- Use storytelling to convey information in the lessons to provide student with an opportunity to visualize the main ideas and help them remember the content.
- Provide access to supplemental computer programs that will provide greater visual exposure and practice.

In addition, more tips, tools, and techniques to try include the following:

- Spelling lists with the words written in different colors
- Mini-flashlights for reading along in text
- Colored acetate strips to cover and highlight text material
- Colored index cards provide visual stimulation and can serve to highlight important facts in various colors
- Transition wheel on board (pie sections: green for working, yellow for getting ready, red for stop)
- Highlighters and highlighter tape
- Advance organizers to capture key ideas
- Symbolic summaries (simple drawings to capture ideas)

- Document camera to focus learning on objects and text
- Colored markers and pencils
- Black-and-white symbols or icons around the room to mark locations for materials
- Photographs or diagrams of proper behavior posted on desk or bulletin board
- Success charts (record of student's successful behaviors)
- Students' best work framed and posted for all to see
- Reminders on corner of student desks
- Secret signal from teacher to cue a student that he or she is about to be called on
- Pictorial behavior or learning contract
- Personal office space with manila folder to block distractions
- Countdown clock on wall to inform student of remaining time
- Color coding for different subjects
- Color coding with highlighters (e.g., red for vocab.)
- Bar or line graphs on which students track their own progress

TIPS FOR VISUAL LEARNERS

> Your brain loves pictures. It's got 20 times the capacity for visual processing as compared to touch, and 60 times that for hearing. So stop talking so much and draw your ideas!

Because visual learners prefer information presented in a written language format or through other visual representations, the following suggestions should be shared with your students who are visual learners to help them succeed in your class:

- Use images, pictures, color, and other visual media to help you learn.
- You may find that visualization comes easily to you.
- Use color, layout, and spatial organization in your associations, and use many "visual words" in your writing.
- Use mind maps, colors, and pictures in place of text whenever possible.
- You have good spatial sense, which gives you a good sense of direction.
- System diagrams can help you visualize the links between parts of a system or a story.
- Replace words with pictures, and use color to highlight major and minor connections.
- The visual journey or story technique helps you memorize content that isn't easy to "see."
- Study in a place that has limited distractions.
- Capture mental images as you take notes in class.
- Use sticky-notes to code text for key ideas.
- To help with comprehension, close your eyes and visualize it first.
- Use different colors of highlighting to help you remember different ideas from a text.
- When hearing a key vocabulary word, visualize its spelling.
- Watch supplemental videos covering topics that you are learning about in class.

INCLUSION STRATEGIES FOR VISUAL LEARNERS

"QUICK DRAW" TECHNIQUES

Overview

Symbolic summaries are "quick draws" that enable children to show what they have learned using visual images. The symbolic summaries strategy is very similar to "Sketch to Stretch" (Harste, Short, & Burke, 1988), an effective reading comprehension strategy in which students quickly sketch key elements of a story or other text selection and then share their drawings. This process stretches their thinking and understanding of concepts.

This technique can be used in a variety of ways, including during teacher read-alouds or partner reading. When using during teacher read-alouds, pause frequently during the story or reading of informational text and ask the students to draw a quick sketch (no more than 30 seconds) of what was memorable to them. This is done after teacher modeling, so that the students realize that the process is not about being a "great artist."

Similarly, this technique can be used with learning partners by having students take turns reading brief passages, doing a quick sketch, and sharing sketches with their partners. The sketches can represent key ideas, details, the most important point, or what they found memorable. This strategy really enhances the visual learner's comprehension of text and fosters interpretive discussions.

Implementation

When students reflect on the reading and decide what to sketch, they are "stretching" their higher-level thinking skills as they:

- Summarize.
- Get the main idea.
- Identify themes.
- Make inferences.
- Look at cause and effect.
- Draw conclusions.
- Create analogies.
- Make comparisons.

When they share their sketches, it is interesting for partners to respond before the sketchers explain their ideas. This exchange can elicit a deeper discussion and further understanding.

Variations: Methods of using this strategy in other ways include the following:

- "Sketch to stretch" **(Hoyt, 1999)** can also be used as a prereading strategy that taps into students' background knowledge about a topic. In this way,

Box continues on next page

the students make a sketch about something they know about the topic or something that they predict that the selection will be about.

- Another variation is to integrate writing into the strategy by asking students to describe the meaning of their sketches in words, with phrases, or using a quote from the text. They can also write an explanation of why they drew what they did.
- As a small-group activity, students can read a passage and each student in the group will sketch a different idea as it is sequenced in the story or chapter, paying attention to the events at the beginning, middle, and end and the necessary details in between.
- Although this technique is most frequently used as a post-reading strategy, students could also create sketches while they are reading to help them connect with the text and to support close reading.

Challenges

Some students might have difficulty moving from the concrete words, ideas, and themes in the text or story to an abstract, symbolic summary. That is why teacher modeling and continued support is critical to the success of this strategy.

FOCUS ON YOUR WORK

Visual learners are easily distracted by competing visual stimuli. Tactile, kinesthetic, and auditory learners may also find it difficult to attend to paperwork on their desks.

Book Lights

Small battery-powered reading lights may be attached to a student's book or to a clipboard. The beam of light projected on the book's surface helps the student focus on the words on the page.

Penlights

Penlights are available at office supply stores. Students who have difficulty tracking print will enjoy using these novel tools as they read or follow along.

HIGHLIGHTER TAPE

Overview

Highlighter tape provides extra visual input to students and gives your tactile learners opportunities to physically interact with printed text. This type of highlighting material is transparent, adheres to paper without damaging it, and may be used and reused to accent sections of text.

Implementation

Vinyl adhesive book covers may also be cut easily into shapes and used to draw students' attention to specific parts of a page. These bright covers may be obtained at office supply stores or ordered by calling Kittrich Corporation, 1-800-321-1741. I recommend cutting them into shapes like arrows that serve as pointers when placed on a page that the student is reading. The arrows are visual clues on where to start reading.

Several lengths of highlighter tape may be placed on index cards; each student can keep one of these index cards at his or her desk and can use the pieces of highlighter tape to accent sections of text, such as main ideas, important points, critical dates, unknown words, and confusing information.

INDIVIDUAL RESPONSE BOARDS

Overview

Individual white boards and individual chalkboards are wonderful tools in inclusive classrooms. They enable visual learners to temporarily escape the limitations of pencil and paper. The every-pupil-response technique ensures student engagement and keeps visual learners focused on the task.

Implementation

Ideas for using individual response boards include the following:

- Math—facts, computations, story problems
- Reading—letter formation, sound–letter correspondence
- Spelling—accuracy, correct word usage
- Content-area studies—facts, opinions, vocabulary

SURPRISE BAGS

"Surprise bags" are brightly colored drawstring bags that lend an element of novelty and surprise to the classroom. In this strategy, these "mystery" bags (or colorful pillowcases with a drawstring added to the open end) hide some sort of object(s) that will be used in the lesson to come. Teachers might use it as an activator at the beginning of a lesson by describing the object verbally and having the students guess what is inside the bag before it is revealed. This ignites the students' sense of wonder and is an excellent strategy to foster predictions and create a "need to know." The visual learners are excited to see what emerges from the bag.

Adapted from Beninghof, 1998

BRAND-NAME PHONICS

Make a different kind of word wall for your visual learners. Gather a collection of empty boxes of cereal, toothpaste boxes, and other wrappers and mount them on the wall. This word wall comes to life when you have the students interact with it by finding, for example, "words that have a short *e* sound" or "words that rhyme with _____." This is an excellent strategy to bring in environmental print that visual learners quickly recognize and feel successful with.

"WHEEL OF FORTUNE"

In this strategy, the teacher reads aloud a few pages from the end of a story. Pre-selected words from the story are displayed with certain letters deleted (as in the TV game show of the same name). Students then guess letters to fill in the blanks until all of the words are recognized that they heard in the preview reading of the text. Pictures are not shown so that students visualize the words in their minds. Students make predictions about the story based on the ending. Reading of the complete story resumes. Visual learners find this activity of prediction and word study particularly engaging.

SIGHT WORD CONCENTRATION

Follow these instructions for the sight word concentration strategy:

- Print two sets of 10 word bank words on cards, with numbers on the other side.
- Turn over the 10 sight word cards and mix them up.
- Ask each student in turn to flip over a card, say the word on the card, and try to find a match by turning over another card. If there is no match, it is the next player's turn.
- You can also use a pocket chart with the words printed on one side and numbers on the other.
  - ➤ Remind the students to watch so they will know where the words are when it's their turn.
  - ➤ You could also enhance this activity by requiring that the student needs to define the word pair or use it in a sentence to gain the point for the match.

POSSIBLE SENTENCES

Follow these steps to use the possible sentences strategy:

- Select about six words from the text before students read it or before it is used in a read-aloud. Add four words already known by students. You can post these on the board or provide students with handouts. For example:
  - ➤ Mammals, ocean, krill, blowhole, baleen, breech
  - ➤ Large, killer, swim, eat
- Have students make sentences that contain at least two of these words in writing.
- Have students make predictions about what they think the passage will be about based on the vocabulary shared.
- Read the story to or with students. After reading, discuss the sentences and whether they are true given the new information in what they read.

PICTURE SORTS

Overview

The picture sort strategy is a powerful tool to use to promote success for visual learners because it allows students to rely on visual picture cues instead of letters to do their word sorts. This technique is also very meaningful to the successful comprehension of English language learners.

Implementation

Use the following steps to implement picture sorts in the classroom:

- You should prepare at least 15 to 20 cards for this activity.
- Picture cards are sorted according to their initial, medial, or final sound(s). The categories may focus on a single consonant, blend, digraph, or vowel sound.
- Begin by using picture cards as the sort headers (by sound), then progress to letter–picture matching.
- Sort three across and four down. Always use the same pictures as column headers.
- Review the names of the picture cards so they are familiar.
- If a student experiences difficulty and makes a mismatch, read the two words, emphasizing the initial (medial, final) sound. State that these do not have the same sound at the beginning and place the card in the correct column.

Procedure

The picture sort proceeds as follows:

- Give individual students a picture card to sort in the corresponding column. Ask where the picture goes, and ask the rest of the group to read the picture cards in the column, listening for the correct beginning sound. Depending on the ages and ability levels of your students, use as many picture cards as necessary (at least 12 to 15).
  - ➤ Example: "Rake" goes under "ring" because they begin with the same sound.
- For matching to letter card headers: Review the letters and pictures.
  - ➤ For example: "If we were to write the word *sun*, the first letter would be an *s*. The letter *s* stands for the first sound in *sun*. Now let's sort these pictures under the right letter card."
- After each match, take away the picture card that was just placed so that the students attend to the letters, using these as a guide and not another picture.

Concentration: When you have finished sorting the picture cards, students can play concentration with them, matching pictures or letters.

Adapted from Hoyt, 1999

FLIP BOOKS

Overview

After the students complete a reading, they are asked to reflect and connect their ideas to their learning using a flip book. The flip book is a fun, hands-on strategy students can use to summarize main events. This technique provides an alternative to a traditional written book report, and is especially useful for the visual learners. See Figure _____ for flip book examples.

Implementation

Flip books are easily made and require very little preparation. Provide each student with an 8½"×11" sheet of blank paper. Ask them to fold it in half lengthwise, then fold it into fourths. With a pair of scissors, have them cut on the fold to the midpoint crease, creating four flaps.

There are many ways to use a flip book as a summarizer strategy, such as the following:

- *Character description:* Students can draw the main characters of the story on the outside flaps. Underneath the flaps they list the attributes of each character.
- *Story sequencing:* On the outside of the flaps students write the title of the story and the words *beginning, middle,* and *end.* Underneath the flaps students list the main events that happened at the beginning, middle, and end of the story.
- *Story elements:* Students write the words *character, setting, plot,* and *solution* on the outside flaps. Underneath they use words or pictures to depict the essence of these story elements.

ALPHABOX CHART

Overview

The alphabox chart (Hoyt, 1999) can be used in many ways. As a prereading strategy, students use it to predict vocabulary that they might find in the text or story. As a summarizer activity, students can brainstorm with learning partners two words that they think of when they reflect on the story or text. Then the alphaboxes are shared with the whole group. Students can also draw pictures of key words and put them in the "alphabox."

Implementation

Create a grid with 26 squares, with each box labeled with the letters of the alphabet. Alphabet clusters can be used as shown in Figure 5.1, requiring fewer boxes. As the students read, they collect words and place them in the appropriate boxes.

Prereading strategy: Use this as a prereading strategy to activate prior knowledge, set a purpose for reading, or have students connect to text.

Assign a vocabulary term as your focus and ask students to write words this term brings to mind in the appropriate boxes. Discuss the chosen words as a class, with students explaining their choices. Have students make predictions and then read the text.

During reading: Have students read the text (independently, in pairs, etc.) and write words they think are key to the concept being addressed. Students may add page numbers where they found evidence to support and defend their choices. As a class or in groups, discuss word choices as a post-reading activity.

An alternative is to focus on character traits or conflicting ideas by using two different colors to write words on grid. This is a great technique for literature/novel study or concepts in the content areas of science, social studies, and math.

Post-reading: Have students write a persuasive paragraph to convince the teacher or peers of the five most important words to explain the concept or topic. Alternatively, have students write a compare/contrast essay comparing two different characters or opposing ideas in the content area.

To use this strategy as an assessment tool, have students choose the three most important words to explain a concept and defend their answers.

Please note that you should develop a tentative list of terms before beginning the activity to launch the students on their learning, keep them focused, and allow for reasonable suggestions to be made.

Variations: Students can collect words individually, with partners, in small groups or as a whole class. With the words collected in the alphabox, students can create their own word banks related to the topic. Teachers can collect all of the words selected and create a word wall specific to the topic or unit of study.

Adapted from Hoyt, 1999

Figure 5.I. Alphabox Chart

A-B	C-D	E-F
G-E	I-J	K-L
M-N	O-P	Q-R
S-T	U-V	W-X-Y-Z

ART POSTCARD ACTIVITIES

Overview

The use of postcards to promote visual literacy is a powerful strategy. Start your collection of unusual and visually appealing postcards by asking family, friends, and even your students to contribute items. Once your collection is made, they can be used in multiple activities with your visual-literacy and English learners. These activities encourage your students to think divergently and promote their creation of metaphoric connections.

Box continues on next page

Implementation

Large-group activity:

- Each student gets three to six postcards.
- The facilitator puts one random card on the floor and tells the group to start connecting cards to that card, domino style, based on any relationship or connection they can come up with. The activity keeps going until all cards are connected. Because there are no right or wrong answers, the discussion becomes very interesting about connections made. This is an inclusionary activity not only for visual learners, but also struggling readers and English learners.

Small-group activity:

- The facilitator selects four to six cards randomly and gives them to small groups of three or four students. Each group receives four to six cards.
- The task is for each group to make connections and then explain how or why the cards are connected to the whole class. Visual learners often make very interesting connections, and the small-group configuration makes it comfortable for all learners to share their ideas.

Individual-response activity within small groups:

- Students should sit in groups of four or five people.
- Each person gets one postcard and a blank sheet of notebook paper.
- Step 1: each person answers question 1 in either phrases or sentences based on the card he or she was given.
  - ➤ For example: If you could enter the environment of this image, what sounds (even silence) would you hear?
- Step 2: Each student passes the paper and the card clockwise, and each person answers question 2 based on the new card.
  - ➤ For example: What's missing in this picture? What would you add?
- Step 3: Another pass is made and students answer question 3.
  - ➤ For example: Think of all the ways we tell time. What time is in this image?
- Step 4: Another pass is made and students answer question 4.
  - ➤ For example: If you were part of this picture, what would you be doing?
- Step 5: Another pass is made and students answer question 5.
  - ➤ For example: If you were in this picture, where would you be going? Where would you end up?
- Step 6: Another pass is made, returning each card and paper to the original person.
- Step 7: Each student writes a paragraph incorporating all of the responses on the paper (allow about 3–5 minutes).
- Step 8: Either pass the cards around again so everyone can read all of the paragraphs, or leave the pictures and paragraphs at the desks or tables and students can circulate around and read them.
- Follow-up question: How did this activity broaden your perspective or change the way you view images? Did you learn anything new about yourself?

COMPREHENSION CODING

Overview

Students are encouraged to interact with the text as they read a selection by circling unknown words, putting question marks in the margin, making predictions, and underlining key ideas. The INSERT Strategy (Interactive Notation System to Effective Reading and Thinking) was developed by Vaughn and Estes (1986) as an active reading strategy. It is particularly useful for less skilled readers to help them clarify issues as they read. If students have their own books and can mark in them it is very helpful. However, sticky notes can be used effectively to code the text, or students can use a separate sheet of paper or use strips of paper in the margin as they read.

Implementation

Follow these steps to use the coding strategy in the classroom:
- Describe the coding strategy to students and how it can be helpful to their comprehension of and connection with the text.
- Demonstrate and model the use of the technique using a think-aloud process as you read the text to the class.
- Develop a classroom coding system (see accompanying lists).
- Guide students in using the coding strategy and discussing their thinking as they read along.
- Have students practice in pairs or small groups by reading and coding small segments of text and then comparing and contrasting their marks and how they coded the passages.
- Support independent work using the coding strategy after pairs, small groups, or the whole class has practiced coding.
- Discuss with the students how this strategy helped them read, remember, and connect with text.

Insert Marking System

$\times$ I think differently
+ This is new information
/ I agree
= An answer to a question
! Wow!
? I don't understand a word or idea
* Important to remember

Comprehension Codes

MI Main Idea
V Vocabulary
PD Prediction
PC Personal Connection
D Discoveries

VISUALIZATION—USING MENTAL IMAGERY

> "Good readers often form mental pictures, or images, as they read. Readers who visualize during reading understand and remember what they read better than readers who do not visualize . . . urge them to picture a setting, character or event described in the text" (Put Reading First, 2000).
>
> Readers use their five senses to help experience the story—"like a movie in my head."
>
> Proficient readers use images to draw conclusions, create unique interpretations of the text, recall significant details, and retell a text after it has been read (Miller, 2005).

MODEL: THINK ALOUD THROUGH THE TEXT TOGETHER

Follow these steps to model the think-aloud strategy:

- Think aloud and describe the images that come to mind as you read an important part of the story or a poem. For example, vivid scenes of gardens, animals, or food may inspire mental images linked to prior experiences—explain that you are creating pictures in your head as you read.
- Next, use the following dialogue or something similar:
  - ➢ Close your eyes, and listen to the words as I read.
  - ➢ Pay attention to the images that come alive in your mind.
  - ➢ What is your brain telling you? Imagine that you are really there.
  - ➢ Put your thumb up when an image comes into your head.
  - ➢ Share this image (e.g., "I could picture. . .," "I could [hear, smell, taste]. . .").
- Prompt with a green cue card. Ask questions that encourage details and uniqueness.
- Reaffirm that each person's image will be different because our past experiences and knowledge (schemas or mental files) are all different.

OPEN-MIND PORTRAIT

In this strategy, students draw and color a portrait of a character or famous person from a biography. Follow these steps to implement the strategy:

- Each student cuts out the portrait and uses it to trace blank head shapes on several sheets of paper.
- Inside the head shapes, they are to draw or write about the chosen person's thoughts and feelings throughout the text.
- Share the open-mind portraits as a class.
- As a variation, have students use a double-entry journal format—Mind Portrait/Alternative Mind Portrait—to illustrate two differing points of view or perspectives in the text.

WHAT DO I SEE? WHAT DO I THINK? WHAT DO I WONDER?

"Illustrations are as important as—or more important than—the text in conveying a message" (Anderson, 2002).

Overview

See–think–wonder (STW) is a visual literacy strategy that helps emergent readers focus on the text illustrations and promotes higher-order thinking and problem-solving abilities. This activity provides motivation for reading and helps readers make predictions about the goals, actions, and personal traits of the characters. It enables successful participation by all students.

Implementation

To implement the STW strategy, follow these steps:
- *Display the front cover of a book* with a vivid illustration that depicts some of the characters, setting, and events.
- Tell students they are going to learn a new strategy called What Do I See? What Do I Think? What Do I Wonder? that will help them *look carefully at the pictures* and think about the *story's characters, settings, and events*.
- Draw student attention to one facet of the illustration and *model the strategy* of responding to the prompts in a chart like that shown in Figure 5.2.

Figure 5.2. See–Think–Wonder Chart

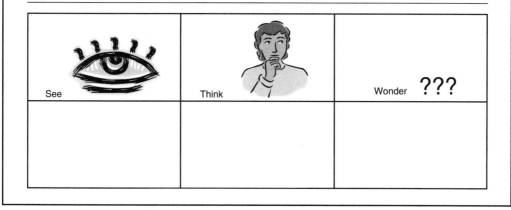

MENTAL ENERGY—LIKE A MOVIE IN YOUR HEAD

Overview

Comprehension is enhanced when students create visual images in their minds as they read.

Box continues on next page

Implementation

Choose a group member to read the *first half* of the story aloud. The group readers *do not show the group the pictures,* and pause at intervals to allow the other group members time to draw and record their most vivid images on sticky notes. Students place these on the second column of a chart like that shown in Figure 5.3, with the corresponding text phrase or reference in the first column.

The group readers then reread the first half of the story, this time showing the pictures. Students compare the actual images with the ones they created.

The readers now read the rest of the story *without showing the pictures,* pausing as they read so the other group members can *draw and record* further images, again placing these on the second column of the chart and the corresponding text phrase or reference in the first column. Discuss how the images from the second reading have incorporated more information from the story and how showing, not telling, in writing is linked to visualizing.

Figure 5.3. Chart for Mental Imagery Strategy

Quote from the Text	What I Visualize

SNAPSHOT SENTENCES

Overview

Students read a passage of informational text that contains descriptive details written to evoke visual images. Students then create "snapshot sentences" that capture the sensory details and figurative language of the text. Visual learners benefit from these sequential images that anchor the main ideas of the text in visual form.

Implementation

Follow these steps to implement the snapshot sentences strategy:

- Have students create snapshot sentence summaries using descriptive details and sketches from reading selections of an informational text.
- Collect snapshot summaries from several students that represent different text selections. Have students categorize and sort the summaries, noting similarities and differences.
- Invite students to add snapshot sentences that help them visualize the author's main ideas.
- Take students outside for "field observations" to create on-the-spot sensory snapshot summaries. You can use the following prompts:
  - ➤ What do you see?
  - ➤ What do you smell?
  - ➤ What sounds do you hear?
  - ➤ How does the air feel?

CHAPTER 6

Graphic Organizers
Making Thinking Visible

WHAT IS A GRAPHIC ORGANIZER?

Graphic organizers come in many sizes, shapes, and configurations and are strategic learning tools to use in classroom instruction. Essentially, they are visual representations of students' learning and provide an alternative that allows struggling readers to display their learning in a different way. They guide the students' thinking as they fill in and build upon a visual diagram. Graphic organizers provide a means for structuring information, showing connections between topics, and arranging qualities and characteristics of a concept, topic, or character. They depict the relationships between facts and ideas within a learning task.

Many different structures and designs for graphic organizers are effectively utilized in classrooms today—the choice of format depends on the desired learning outcomes and the content. Some of the types of graphic organizers include the following: mind maps, concept maps, Venn diagrams, story maps, word webs, fishbone diagrams, network maps, the compare–contrast matrix, and others.

Graphic organizers can be used at the prereading phases, during reading to keep track of key ideas, as well as in the post-reading stage. In addition, graphic organizers can be used effectively in prewriting, discussion, and note-taking. They are important summary and synthesis tools for struggling readers and English learners because they allow students to actually see the relationships and key ideas rather than just imagining them or listing them in rote fashion, such as through an outline. Graphic organizers provide an overview of information in abbreviated fashion rather than in lengthy narrative, sequential, or expository format.

The visual appeal of graphics on worksheets encourages students to put pen to paper. Images stimulate thinking, and graphs and diagrams help students to organize their thoughts. Graphic organizers serve well in lesson follow-up activities as well as in prewriting activities.

Visual Learning Improves Performance

As discussed in the previous chapter, visual learning techniques are effective methods to modify the curriculum and improve the performance of many struggling students in the classroom. A strong research base and solid evidence support the use of graphic organizers as a means for students to conceptualize their cognitive frameworks and improve retention and comprehension of material covered in classroom instruction.

Graphic organizers have been used with a variety of content areas and have verified applications in math, science, social studies, language arts, and technical fields. This form of visual learning helps students clarify and synthesize their thoughts. The mapping of key concepts and visually organizing cause and effect as well as comparison and contrast can be beneficial in many subject areas and across multiple grade levels with diverse learners. Students begin to make connections and can visualize how information can be grouped and organized. Because of this, new concepts are more easily understood and linked to prior knowledge.

> The beneficial effects in multiple subject areas have been verified to increase reading comprehension and vocabulary development. Evidence of the positive learning outcomes of using graphic organizers has been thoroughly investigated by numerous studies (e.g., Bulgren, Schumaker, & Deshler, 1988; Idol, & Croll, 1987; Merkley & Jeffries, 2001).

Furthermore, graphic organizers make assignments easier to access for students, especially when they have a lot of information to organize. With graphic organizers, students start with a lot of information and then narrow the focus by eliminating unnecessary details to get to the essential ideas. These visual clues are helpful to students in organizing their writing (Alvermann & Boothby, 1986).

Introducing Graphic Organizers

Graphic organizers can be applied successfully throughout a range of subject areas and grade levels. They are easily adapted in an inclusive classroom. Primary students can use graphic organizers to break down big ideas for easier communication. In addition to facilitating students to organize their thoughts and writing, they are an effective instructional technique to illustrate their knowledge about a topic. As a teaching tool, they help students compare ideas in a format that they can relate to. Older students can use them as an effective brainstorming tool to organize their ideas.

The steps or procedures to implement this strategy are as follows:

1. Determine the topic or concept that will be the subject of students' visual representations.
2. Select which graphic organizer will best suit the topic and organize the information.
3. Model the concept for the students by filling in the elements of the selected graphic organizer for a similar topic.
4. Engage students in gathering the information for their graphic organizers.
5. Share the results and add additional details.

Further explanation of these steps is as follows:

1. As noted, graphic organizers can be used in a variety of ways across all grade levels and content areas, including simple brainstorming for a writing task, outlining, or story sequencing. As an instructional tool for your struggling readers, you will need to establish the selected topics, sub-categories, and details that support the topic.
2. Once the topic has been established, pose questions such as "Which graphic organizers fit this topic best?" or "How can my students best represent and record the information in graphic form?" You may want to select several approaches so that students are provided a variety of representations.
3. After the graphic format has been established, teachers should assign the reading and model the use of the organizer. Modeling the process is critical to student success.
4. Once your students have demonstrated comfort and success with using graphic organizers—set them loose! Working with learning partners is a great way to begin for struggling readers and English learners. While they are working, be sure to circulate and monitor as they are completing their organizers. This can help catch potential confusions, especially if the students are reluctant to ask for help.
5. Please keep in mind that graphic organizers are only tools to provide information in a visual format—they are not the end product of student learning. Once the information has been recorded, there should be a student–teacher discussion to see if any essential information is missing or not sufficiently covered to explain the topic.

Structured dialogue is the key to the powerful use of these organizers and includes the following:

- Clear demonstration of the need/value/use of these visual enhancements
- Clear modeling of the thinking involved; interactive dialogue with students as you fill out a graphic organizer as a model; working together; thinking aloud
- Verbal elaboration by the students—explaining the graphic organizer to a learning partner; explaining their understanding, comparing and contrasting differences, and so forth

In addition, the consider the following when using this strategy:

- Align your assessments and evaluation (e.g., tests, quizzes, writing assignments) to the key ideas and concepts depicted in the diagrams/maps/graphics.
- Value the student thinking involved—not just whether they have all of the facts.

- Provide many opportunities to work with other students in a variety of cooperative learning structures.
- Make sure that students have many opportunities to explain the graphic to someone else and elaborate on the ideas, such as using the organizer as a writing prompt. The "magic" of graphic organizers is in their use and application to learning.

Extending Mapping Strategies

The use of graphic organizer strategies can help students consolidate and elaborate on their understanding of what's been read. These strategies are usually best done in small collaborative teams using the principles of structured cooperative learning. The goal is to get students to process the information at a deeper and more meaningful level. This in turn will facilitate increased retention and recall.

Some options for extending the strategy include having students do the following:

1. Revisit old maps and add/delete information.
2. Add small symbols/graphics that form associations with prior knowledge.
3. Verbally explain the maps to someone else.
4. Use the maps to structure "debate organizers" to take sides on an issue and have a debate.
5. Use different or more complex maps to analyze maps more deeply.
6. Use the maps as prewriting organizers prior to writing assignments on related topics.

INSTRUCTIONAL APPLICATIONS

Attribute Charts

Students explore specific attributes related to a topic. After students complete the reading of an informational text passage, they construct an attribute chart to help them visually organize the details. The grid provides a visual framework with category headings in the top horizontal row of the chart. The topic headings are then placed in the left-hand column. Students are asked to review the passage to collect details for the grid. They then fill in the facts on the chart. This also works well as a partner activity to share ideas.

CONCEPT MAPS

Overview

Similar to an attribute chart, a concept map or web helps to organize ideas about a specific topic in a visual format. Concept maps are an effective instructional strategy that can be used before, during, or after the reading to check for understanding.

As a prereading experience, students brainstorm qualities, characteristics, and ideas they have about a central idea or topic. This process taps into their background knowledge and can be used as a formative assessment tool by the teacher to determine the students' ideas about a topic before launching into a unit of study.

The concept maps can be added to with additional details as the students collect new information during reading. The maps can also be used as a synthesis activity to summarize the main ideas of the lesson.

Implementation

Students write the central main idea of the unit or focus of study in the center of the paper. They write ideas around the central topic in spokes like a web. The teacher should model this first as a whole-group activity before the students do it independently or with learning partners. The students continue by adding further details to the web of ideas. This process activates and assesses students' prior knowledge. Students should revisit their maps to add, change, and extend details collected during further research and reading. This visual memory technique assists with the retention and comprehension of material by visual learners.

Variations

Have students create their own concept maps during a unit of study by adding appropriate illustrations for the details depicted. Students can then use these maps as important visual tools to synthesize the information learned.

WORD WEBS

Overview

Word webs are similar to concept maps. In this strategy, students generate a web of synonyms that each describe a vocabulary word that is at the center of the web.

Implementation

A key vocabulary word is placed in the center of the web. Synonyms for the word and/or descriptors are then added as web extensions and offshoots from the central word. Other ideas for the web include definitions, antonyms, parts of speech, word-in-context sentences, and related themes.

Box continues on next page

Variations

The class can be divided into small groups. Each group creates a different word web for the same word based on distinct categories—for example, definitions, synonyms, context sentences, antonyms, and so forth. The groups can refer to the text for additional information. Upon completion, the various word webs can be displayed around the room to aid students' visual memory.

Students can also create word riddles based on the word webs that are collected. To answer the riddles, the students need to refer to the clues that are posted in the webs around the room.

Use this framework when introducing graphic organizers to your students. This framework is helpful to use in guided practice and modeling (see Figure 6.1).

Figure 6.1. Creating Graphic Organizers

1. Select information/material.

2. Determine facts/concepts.

3. Arrange in a logical manner.

Formats		
	____	Compare/contrast
	____	Concept diagram
	____	Central idea diagram

Specific to content	____	Considerations
Placement of material	____	
Reference points	____	

4. Prepare Organizer.

In providing initial guided practice with graphic organizers, both teachers and students are involved in the instructional sequence. Figure 6.2 describes what teachers and students should be doing in creating graphic organizers.

Figure 6.2. Modeling Graphic Organizers

A graphic organizer is a visual and/or spatial display of information connected in a meaningful way and can be used by students and teachers for all of the following.

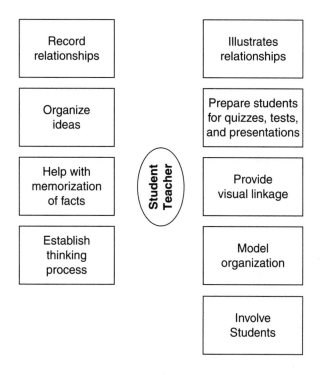

There are many different ways to organize ideas (see figure 6.3). Be sure to model each of these diagrams for the students before using them in a lesson.

Figure 6.3. Graphic Organizers: Frames to Organize Thinking

Select a template that will help your students understand the critical concepts/ideas/relationships of the topic being studied.

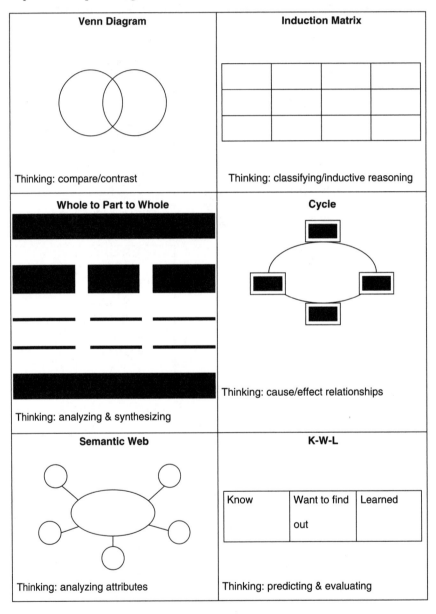

CHAPTER 7

Kinesthetic Strategies
Moving on to Meaning

WHO IS THE KINESTHETIC LEARNER?

For kinesthetic learners, learning takes place most successfully when they actually carry out a physical activity, rather than listening to a lecture or watching a demonstration. These learners are also commonly known as the "doers" in your classroom. Students associated with this learning style are thought to be natural discovery learners. They make up about 15% of the population and struggle to internalize information by reading/listening to things, preferring active rather than passive activities (Coffield, Moseley, Hall, & Ecclestone, 2004).

Research supports the association of spatial awareness and kinesthetic learning with cognitive growth. The more senses that are used for learning, the greater the retention of content will be. Activities such as balancing, jumping, and spinning stimulate the brain to higher functioning (Hannaford, 1995; Jensen, 2000).

This chapter will provide you with practical "hands-on strategies" to use in the classroom to maximize success. Using the body to learn in an inclusive classroom is an efficient and effective way for all students to learn and remember content. Movement in the classroom provides both teacher and students with a stimulating classroom environment and an opportunity to grow physically, emotionally, and socially.

There have been numerous studies regarding the attention spans of students. Kinoshita (1997) found that students who were inactive and sedentary for longer than 20 minutes experienced a decline in neural transmissions in the brain. Furthermore, integrating movement into our lesson plans helps to integrate the two spheres of the brain and improve concentration (Dennison & Dennison, 1988). Research also found a meaningful difference in reading, spelling, and math performance following exercise (Jensen, 2000).

ADVANTAGES OF MOVEMENT TO INCREASE LEARNING

Specific and directed physical movement helps to prepare students' brains for learning and increases brain functions. Physical movement can influence the way students think, learn, and remember, and strengthen their ability to pay attention (Kuczala & Lengel, 2010). Try some of these strategies for a brain-friendly and inclusive classroom. Educating the child as a whole goes beyond just teaching content. Other advantages include:

- Increases circulation
- Provides sensory engagement
- Provides a necessary brain break and state change
- Helps to differentiate instruction for diverse learners
- Focuses students' attention
- Motivates students to participate
- Reduces seat time
- Enhances brain functions

WHAT TO LOOK FOR . . .

Kinesthetic learners learn best by moving their bodies, activating their large or small muscles as they learn. These are the "hands-on learners" or the "doers" who actually concentrate better and learn more easily when movement is involved. These students learn best by doing and direct involvement. They like to try things out and manipulate objects. When speaking, they often use gestures to convey their message. These students, who may not be very attentive during auditory presentations, use movement to help them concentrate. They may need to take "brain breaks" while studying and get up and move around.

WHAT TO DO . . .

The following will help the kinesthetic learners in your classroom:

- Allow students to try things out and put into practice what they have learned.
- Show them how to do things.
- Provide time for quieting down after physical activities.
- Allow for planned time for movement, such as monitoring jobs.
- Create simulations of concepts and allow students to perform them step by step.
- Have students clap or tap out syllables or walk the patterns of words.
- Use screen spelling (described earlier in this book).
- Create "human graphs" for a topic by having students line up to represent the data.
- Have available and use hands-on supplies and activities, such as various drawing materials, clay, models, puzzles, globes and maps, and blocks and cubes.
- Provide students with hands-on learning opportunities that involve physical movement, such as experiments, field trips, role-playing, projects, and games.

Challenges

Kinesthetic learners can quickly become bored when there is not physical movement in the learning process. Therefore, these students often become fidgety and may appear distracted, which can lead to an increase in noise level in the classroom and a loss of focus for the entire class.

Some other challenges include:

- Lecture style classes without the opportunity for questions or discussion
- Teachers who do not allow students to stretch or stand during a long presentation
- Teaching a skill without the opportunity to practice
- Without a hands-on element in the lesson, difficulty in focusing

Ideas for Kinesthetic Learners

Try the following ideas for kinesthetic learners in your classroom:

- Allow students to work on chart paper on the wall or provide standing workstations (places around the room where students are allowed to stand while they work).
- Have students stand, stretch, and cross the midline as a brain break or have them spin after responding and then return to work.
- Use a Koosh-ball or Frisbee toss (throw from student to student; whoever catches must answer or participate).
- Use a sound ball (throw information around the room).
- Provide a beach ball seat (partially inflated beach ball as seat cushion that allows movement without being out of seat).
- Use the beach ball bounce for answering questions.
- Inside-outside circles: divide students into two groups and have them form an inner and outer circle, facing peers. Students rehearse content with the facing peers, then either the outer or inner circle turns, so that each student is matched with new peer (Kagan, Kagan, & Kagan, 2000).
- Select a kinesthetic learner as a resource manager; he or she can collect papers, sharpen pencils, or do other tasks for the teacher or classmates.
- Have students stand to answer questions or when responding in a discussion.
- Let them clap or tap syllables or numbers.
- Have students work with magnets on a metal file cabinet to manipulate information physically.
- Provide breaks for tensing and then relaxing the muscles, helpful for self-control and muscle stimulation.
- Provide a daily stretch break (e.g., hands above head, stretch to one side)

SPECIFIC KINESTHETIC STRATEGIES

STAND IN RESPONSE

Overview

This is an "activator" strategy that you can use when introducing a topic, starting a new lesson, or beginning a unit of study. Think of statements that the students can relate to. They could include personal characteristics as well as academic content. This is a time for the kinesthetic learners to be able to stand up for what they believe in, characteristics that make them unique, and qualities that they might share with others. Celebrating differences and similarities is an important concept in an inclusive classroom.

This is a spontaneous activity in which the teacher states a quality, characteristic, or opinion/fact about the topic. The students then jump up and shout "just like me" if it is a quality, characteristic, or opinion that they believe in. They will look around the room and see who shares in their opinion.

Implementation

The following prompts will help get you started: "Stand up if. . .

- . . . you agree with that statement."
- . . . you have an opinion about this."
- . . . you'd like to explain this to the group."
- . . . you have used a microscope before."
- . . . you identify with the main character."
- . . . you are finished with your work."
- . . . you have a birthday this month."
- . . . you know the main idea of the passage."
- . . . you are left-handed."

VOTING WITH YOUR FEET

Overview

Voting with Your Feet (Beninghof, 1998) is an active, kinesthetic strategy that gets your students up and moving as they express their opinions about a particular topic. This is an excellent needs assessment strategy to use at the beginning of a lesson. Beforehand, you can post signs in the corners of your classroom: "strongly agree," "agree," "disagree," "strongly disagree," and "uncertain." You then state an opinion, and students move to the chosen location to indicate their agreement/disagreement. They discuss with their peers their reasons for their opinions and why they chose the selections that they did. A group discussion follows. This is an instant way for the teacher to glean the opinions of the class and to move forward with instruction. It is active, engaging, and requires the students to not only move, but to substantiate their opinions. In this way, it provides opportunities for students to learn about one another and their preferences and to respect individual differences.

As an activator, this strategy helps students get energized about a topic and interested in learning more about it. For the teacher, it is an excellent needs assessment opportunity to gather information about the students' prior knowledge and ways of thinking about a topic. Voting with Your Feet can introduce a topic to the class and provide students with an opportunity to discuss issues with others who might agree or disagree with them. As a summarizer, this strategy provides an opportunity for students to summarize key points to remember.

This strategy fits well in a differentiated classroom because it gets students of all abilities thinking and doing. Higher-level thinking skills are fostered when a teacher asks a question that has no single right answer. The question becomes an invitation for the students to think and engage their minds to consider alternatives. By inviting them to get out of their seats and move to a certain area of the room, the teacher has engaged the students' bodies as well. Struggling readers and English learners benefit from hearing the opinions of others because it builds oral language, develops their thought processes, and extends their knowledge about a topic.

Implementation

Use the following steps to implement this strategy:

1. Select a topic and then craft statements that allow students to choose "sides" on the topic. For instance, "Students should only watch television programs that their parents agree to. Do you agree or disagree?" The students then physically move to the area representing their choice and discuss opinions with others (the choices are usually posted on signs, one in each corner of the room).

2. Students select one of the alternatives and record it on a piece of paper. It is helpful for students to decide on the choice and put it in writing, independently at their desks before moving.

3. Tell the students that they should move to one side of the room if they agree with the statement and to the other side of the room if they disagree with the statement. You might also include signs for "strongly agree" and "strongly disagree" as well as "uncertain" for older students. Students join others in the class who made the same choices as they did. Have the students practice paraphrasing the reasons for the choices shared by their peers.

5. In the corners, give the students a specific time period to do a pair/share about the reasons for making the choices. Students can pair again for further discussion.

6. Then have students do a pair/share with a student at the opposite side of the room with a differing opinion. Again, each shares the reason for the selection and listens to the other's opinion. Have students practice paraphrasing what their peers have shared.

7. Students then return to their seats. A spokesperson from each corner shares reasons with the class. The teacher engages the students in a whole-class discussion about the different opinions and the reasons each corner was selected (Perez, 2008).

SEQUENCING

Overview

Sequencing is an important comprehension skill to learn at all grade levels. This sequencing strategy involves hands-on techniques and movement for the kinesthetic learner.

Depending on the content area or subject matter, the teacher decides on the facts and events of a lesson. The teacher writes these facts or events on cards and distributes the cards to the students in random order. The students then arrange themselves in chronological order that represents when these events took place or the correct order of the facts.

Implementation

There are many ways that this strategy can be applied and used in different content areas, including the following:

- Sequencing facts in a chapter
- Sequencing events in a story
- Sequencing historical events
- Sequencing the steps in a process

JUMP TO IT!

Overview

You can make a hop-step mat (Beninghof, 1998) by drawing a grid on an inexpensive plastic shower curtain liner. Make sure the squares are large enough for a child's foot to land squarely within them. Place the mat on the floor and have the children gather around it. The teacher provides a question for the students to answer, and they take turns jumping to the correct location on the mat. For example, in a lesson on math facts, you could ask the student to hop on the square representing the answer to 3 + 3, and the student would need to hop into a square that has a 6. Students can also "answer with a jump" by spelling words if the squares contain letters rather than numbers. For instance, you could ask a student to spell *bat*. The student would then jump in the squares with the correct letter in the proper order, one at a time: B—A—T. The shower curtain mat folds up easily and can be stored in your closet for next time.

Implementation

The hop-step mat works well with the following content:

- Letters:
  - ➢ Letter recognition
  - ➢ Sound–letter correspondence
  - ➢ Spelling words
- Numbers:
  - ➢ Number recognition
  - ➢ Addition, subtraction, multiplication, and division facts
- Colors:
  - ➢ Color recognition
- Rhyming words
- Opposites

PODIUM WORKSTATIONS

Overview

Some students have physical difficulty sitting still for long periods of time and lose their concentration. Their need to move may cause them to fidget in their seats and distract the students around them. Standing workstations (Beninghof, 1998) provide relief for children who become uncomfortable in chairs and children who desperately need some acceptable out-of-seat options.

You can easily set up optional podium workstations at strategic locations around the classroom. These can be music stands borrowed from your music teacher, or you can have the students use the tops of file cabinets. Portable podiums also work well for this technique.

Implementation

Students may use these podium stands to do their work independently and will not disturb others. These opportunities to stand and process their work provide a simple way to meet some of your students' kinesthetic needs. This process gets them up and moving instead of in the passive sedentary stance of traditional desks.

STICKY-NOTE SORT/GRAFFITI BOARD

Overview

This is an active brainstorming strategy that involves your entire class in the discussion of a particular topic or issue. You pose an open-ended question related to the lesson, and everyone needs to respond on their sticky notes. Give your students adequate "think time." They can respond with a word, a phrase, or even a picture—that is why this strategy is so powerful for struggling readers.

Students then place the sticky notes in clusters on a blackboard, white board, bulletin board, or large sheet of chart paper. This is an alternative to a traditional brainstorming activity and engages all learners. Many times when teachers ask an open-ended question, the same hands go up again and again and many reluctant learners do not respond. I like to give students time to share with learning partners before posting their "sticky notes" on the graffiti board. Each student has an equal opportunity to contribute his or her opinions in a nonthreatening way. The sticky notes on the board are "anonymous," so students do not need to be concerned about getting the "right" answer or worry about spelling issues. It is a powerful way to build background knowledge about a topic and to check for understanding. There is little preparation involved, and the results are incredible in terms of the number of ideas generated in such a short period of time.

Implementation

Use the following steps to implement this strategy in the classroom:

1. Begin by selecting a topic or an open-ended prompt or question to pose to the students. For example, you could ask: "What do you know about the Civil War?" Write the prompt or question on a sheet of poster paper or on the white board. This will become the "graffiti board" where all responses are harvested.
2. Have the students jot down their response on sticky notes. This response can be in the form of a word, phrase, or picture.
3. Ask the students to share their responses with their learning partners.
4. After the students have had a chance to discuss their responses, designate one of the learning partners to place both sticky notes on the graffiti board (e.g., the tallest partner, the partner with the curliest hair, etc.).
5. Review the multiple responses with the class and discuss themes that emerge. Ask the students how to categorize their responses. This helps build the critical thinking skills of analysis and synthesis. Invite the students to take a "gallery walk" to view all of the individual responses at recess or break to learn more.

As an activator activity, this technique provides an excellent way to build, extend, and enrich the students' background knowledge about a topic. It provides an opportunity for them to become more focused on the topic and sets a purpose for their learning. From a teacher's perspective, this strategy is an excellent way to do a "hands-on" needs assessment of what the students know about a topic or issue before beginning a lesson.

When used as a summarizer technique, students are asked to reflect on the topic or unit that was taught. Provide them with a prompt or a question related to the topic. After they write their responses, you can review these on the graffiti board and quickly assess their level of understanding of the topic (Perez, 2008).

WALL CHARTS

Overview

Wall charts give students an opportunity to work on their feet rather than at their desks. Post chart paper around the room with different sentence stems related to the topic that you are studying. The students work in small groups responding to the prompt on the chart. There is a finite amount of time for them to respond to the prompt before a signal is provided for them to move on to the next chart and add their ideas to it. Depending on the topic, the response time to add to the chart is usually 6 to 8 minutes. This strategy is also known as "carousel brainstorming."

When the students have completed their circuit of charts, they return to the "home-base" chart where they started, review the comments of their peers, and circle the top three ideas to share with the larger group.

Implementation

Wall charts can be implemented for the following activities, among others:

- Brainstorming any topic
- Gathering information about "what we already know"
- Collecting information about "what we hope to learn"
- Reviewing information on a given topic
- Completing math problems
- Recording information during problem solving
- Recording information during a group report-writing assignment

Line Up and Learn

For this strategy, have students form two parallel lines facing each other. Make sure everyone has a partner directly across from him or her. The lines should be about 2 feet apart—close enough to have a conversation, but not uncomfortably close. This activity involves a rapid exchange of information and movement. It is best done after students have completed a quick-write activity and have written some responses to several questions. One line is designated as the "movers"—they move down one partner after they do their pair-share with the partner across from them. The other line is the "shakers"—they stay in place until they have a new partner and a new question to respond to. The teacher calls out a question, and each partner has 30 seconds each to share an answer with the partner facing them. A signal is given and the line-up shifts. This is a great activity for opinion questions or open-ended questions, so that all students feel comfortable to respond.

BINGO BUDDIES—AUTOGRAPH HUNT

Overview

This is an excellent way for students to connect with each other and helps them overcome initial shyness in a new situation. Tell the students that they are going to do an activity to find out things they might not have known about one another. The teacher develops a "bingo board" or a list of traits and characteristics. The students are instructed to interview each other to find other students to autograph their sheets who have the specified trait or characteristic or who know the answer to a question. You can also use some topics that are content related—for example: "Find someone who can name the steps in the scientific method," or "Find someone who can describe the main character of the story we are reading."

Implementation

Use the following steps to implement this strategy in the classroom.

Before the game:

- Distribute the survey sheets and explain that students are to walk around the room and find people who have the characteristics described on the sheet.
- Students write the name of the students or have the other students sign their names in the blanks provided.
- Ask them to find as many people as possible, using each person's name once.

During the game:

- Begin the game.
- Play music and have the students mix and mingle.
- After about 5 to 10 minutes, stop and have the students return to their seats.

After the game, discuss the following:

- What did you notice about yourself and others during this game?
- Did you learn anything new about someone?
- If you were making up questions for this activity, what are some things you'd like to ask?

Examples of prompts include the following, among others: "Find a bingo buddy who . . . "

- Is wearing the same color as you
- Has visited another state
- Saw a movie this weekend

- Loves to eat pizza
- Has an older brother and sister
- Has a pet
- Has a birthday this month
- Plays a musical instrument
- Speaks a language other than English
- Cooked a meal recently
- Is the oldest in his or her family
- Is wearing jewelry

"Koosh-Ball" Questioning

Kinesthetic students love to catch things—it helps them stay focused. Why not toss a soft or squishy ball around when you are leading a brainstorming session or discussion? It helps all students remain more focused and become more engaged in the process, as they are eager to catch the ball and toss it to someone else. It is a lively alternative to raising their hands to respond. The pace is quick. It is helpful if the teacher does the tossing of the ball to students who are ready to respond. Once the students understand the process, they can proceed to toss it to each other. Different objects can be tossed and responded to as well. Some other choices include throwing Frisbees, small stuffed animals, and other small and lightweight objects.

Word Theater

This is a dynamic way for kinesthetic learners and struggling readers to act out their spelling and vocabulary words. Students take turns and act out the words while the rest of the class guesses what the word is. Students prepare the current vocabulary or spelling words on cards and place them in a bag, then take turns selecting a "secret card" and demonstrating it through actions for the rest of the class. This is an active spelling version of the classic game of charades. For instance, if the key vocabulary word were "airplane," the student might pretend to be flying, with his or her arms outstretched.

Pass the Motion

This is a great activity to do when your students need an energetic break. Have the students form a circle in an open space. Put on some jazzy and lively music. One student starts a motion to the music, and then everyone follows and copies the motion. The motion is then passed around the circle; each student changes the motion in turn. This is the best 3-minute brain break you can do. The students return to work much more focused and ready to learn.

Research confirms that students in stimulating and active environments produce more neural connections in the brain (Bruer, 1991).

SWAP AND SHARE

Overview

This activity can be used as an activator or a summarizer. This is a great structure for review or hooking students into a new lesson. Students put their own ideas in the top three boxes of a grid-like chart. Then, on the teacher's cue, they move about the room asking the other students for one of their ideas. At the same time they give one of their ideas to others. This is done until all the boxes are filled.

The teacher gives the students directions to write three things they know about _____ (the topic that you are studying). They put each of the 3 facts in a separate box. If struggling readers have trouble with words, they can draw pictures in each box. At the end of the lesson, you can use the grids to check for understanding by asking them to write three things they remember about _____ (the topic). The teacher gives the "start" signal to begin. Music can be played in the background as they mix and mingle with their classmates. They share answers from the grid with a partner, and then they swap an answer from the partner's grid. Then they need to move on to a new partner. As an activator, this builds necessary background knowledge in an interactive way. As a summarizer, it is a great way to check for understanding.

This strategy gets everyone up and moving and sharing together in structured academic discussions with peers, before sharing with the whole class.

Implementation

Use the following steps to implement this strategy in the classroom:

- Students can fold a sheet of paper in half lengthwise to form two columns and write "my ideas" at the top of the left-hand column "Ideas from others" at the top of the other column. This is based on the "Give One, Get One" strategy of Kagan. (Kagan et al., 2000).
- Once the students have written down two or three ideas to share, they move around the room and swap their ideas with others, one at a time, adding the new ideas to the grid or list.
- They continue this process until the grid or list is full.
- Remind students to share only one idea with a partner before moving on—this prevents "clumping" together in groups.
- As students brainstorm their individual lists, you can circulate around the room to provide support and ideas to students struggling to come up with ideas on their own.
- Discuss the final lists and ideas with the goal of accuracy and so that everyone has an opportunity to contribute.

GALLERY WALKS ("CHART CHATTER")

Overview

The gallery walk is an activity that allows students to actively generate and display their ideas around the classroom in an interactive way. These shared responses are group projects that are displayed and visited by all groups in the learning community (Kolodner, 2004). This discussion technique gets students out of their seats and into a mode of active engagement. It also allows for formative assessment, as teachers can see students' levels of understanding about topics of study. To set the stage for their learning, discuss the purpose and process of the gallery walk.

Implementation

To implement the strategy in the classroom, follow these steps:

- Place four to six sheets of chart paper around the room on the walls.
- Generate questions. Each chart will contain a different question related to the topic being covered or an open-ended prompt.
- The students form small groups of four to six, decide on a recorder and, with a marking pen, write their responses down.
- Begin the gallery walk: When time is called, they move on to a new chart (new station) and a new question and keep adding their own ideas to the charts as they move.
- The movement continues until all groups have returned to the starting point.
- At the original chart, each group reviews all of the responses from classmates and highlights the three main ideas.
- Report results: These ideas are then shared with the total group.
- Gauge student understanding and challenge misconceptions: While students are reporting key ideas, the teacher is listening for main thoughts and accuracy, reinforcing accordingly. The teacher then considers: What did they find difficult, and how can I modify my instruction to meet their needs?
- Variation: For nonfiction texts, headings on charts could include "Facts," "Questions," and "Responses."

Adapted from Kagan, 1994

Anchor it in Action: Show Me, Don't Tell Me!

When you are teaching a subject, think of ways that you can involve the whole body by coming up with movement or body symbols to help anchor that subject in students' memories. Model the movements and then have the students repeat after you. For example, when you teach multiple intelligences, you demonstrate to the students how this will "stretch" their learning (pretend to be stretching taffy by pulling your hands apart). You will also help them "connect" their learning (bring your hands together and interlock them). Finally, a multiple intelligence lesson will help them to "celebrate" their learning (raise your hands over your hand and wave your hands in the air). As you demonstrate these motions, the students will also copy your gestures for "stretch," "connect," and "celebrate."

SUMMARY "SCRUNCH"

Overview

Research says that if you spend 3 to 5 minutes reflecting on a lesson at its conclusion, student comprehension will be boosted by at least 50%. This activity is one of my favorite for reflecting and summarizing and is very compatible with the kinesthetic learning style. Give each student a blank sheet of paper. Ask them to write down three things they remember from the lesson. Demonstrate scrunching up the paper into a round ball, then ask the students to stand up. At the signal, they are to throw the "scrunch balls" *randomly* and *gently* and then catch someone else's "scrunch ball" to find out what another student remembered from the lesson.

Implementation

The students *love* this activity! I recommend that you do it the last 3 minutes of class or before recess, as they tend to get excited about it. Other prompts you could give them include the following:

- Write down three words you learned today.
- Write down three successes you had today in class.
- Write down three new ideas you learned.
- Write down three questions for homework (whoever catches their "scrunch ball" answers the questions).

The students love the anonymity of this activity and the sense of discovery and mystery.

Adapted from Kagan, 1994

MINDSTREAMING

Overview

This is an exciting mixer and random grouping technique that you can do at a moment's notice. Whenever you think your students need a "brain break" to pause to reflect on what they have learned, ask them to stand up, raise their hands, and then find someone else with their hand up to form a team. Once they have a partner, they wait for directions.

Implementation

Once they have their partners, ask them to decide who is A and who is B, and then use the following steps:

- Tell them that you want to see the hands of the B partner. Say, "B stands for *before* and *begin*, so the Bs will go first."

- The B students are to pretend that their partners just walked in the class right now and missed the entire lesson. They have 30 seconds to share with their partners everything that they found memorable about what was covered.
- Students then switch roles—A students are the talkers and B students are the listeners.
- After the exchange, they can return to their seats.
- This brief exchange lasts no more than 4 minutes, and yet they discover that they have expanded their comprehension about the topic because their partner remembered different aspects of the lesson, which also highlights the benefits of diversity.

WORD CHEERS: ALPHABET ACTIONS!

Overview

This is a way to "act out" the alphabet by having the students pose using motions as they spell out the letters to the word.

Implementation

Use the following steps to implement this strategy in the classroom:

- Print the target high-frequency word on a line on the board or on a chart.
- Point out the configuration of the word produced by the tall letters, the letters that sit on the line, and the letters with tails.
- Have students practice reaching for the sky in a big stretch for the tall letters such as "t" and "h," placing the hands on the hips—the midline—for letters sitting on the line such as "a" and "m," and touching their toes (or as far as they can go) for letters with tails, such as "g" and "y."

When students know the movements, have them chant or cheer the spelling of the word as they do the movement for each letter. Begin by stating the word and end with a rousing cheer as you call out the whole word again. For example: "they—t-h-e-y—they!"

STRETCH IT OUT

Overview

This is an active way to have your students review the key points of a lesson, prepare for a quiz, boost comprehension and retention, and be actively involved as a team to achieve the end goal—the finish line! It is done in a lighthearted manner to reduce pressure and promote teamwork and collaboration.

Implementation

Use the following steps to implement this strategy in the classroom:

1. Gather the students together in a basketball court or any area with lines.
2. Explain ahead of time that the students will be holding hands.
3. Have students assemble in single-file lines of five or more students on the baseline.
4. The teacher goes to the line that is ready first and starts there.
5. Show a flashcard to the first student in the first line. If the student answers correctly, he or she stretches sideways onto the court (heading to the opposite end), keeping one foot on the baseline.
6. If the student is incorrect, he or she goes to the end of the line.
7. The teacher moves along the baseline until every team has had a turn.
8. The teacher then goes back to the first team and gives the next student in line a turn. If this student is correct, he or she locks elbows or hold hands with the student stretching toward the opposite end of the court, forming a chain that stretches down the basketball court. If incorrect, the student goes to the end of the line.
9. If all players are stretched, go to the last player and give him or her a turn. If the student is correct, he or she goes to the front of the line and stretches it out farther. If not, the student stays put until the next turn.
10. Continue the game until one team has stretched to the opposite baseline.
11. Have all teams come to the baseline, reform lines, and play again.

Note: It is a good idea to have a helper to judge the lines while you are asking the questions.

RELAY SPELLING

Overview

This strategy is an active alternative to having students simply write down their spelling or vocabulary words, which is a passive pencil-and-paper act that is not very engaging for your kinesthetic learners. Why not try this as an alternative to engage your students?

Implementation

Use the following steps to implement this strategy in the classroom:

1. Divide students into three or four equal teams.
2. The teams of students will line up directly behind each other, in straight lines.
3. Directly in front of their lines, at a distance determined by the teacher, is a box filled with letters of the alphabet (one letter per card; cards are laminated).
4. The teacher will go to each line (team) and quietly announce the word that is to be spelled and what physical movement will be required to get the job done (e.g., walking, skipping, hopping; see step 3 under Preparation).
5. On a start signal, one member at a time will run to the team's box and find any letter of the spelling word announced by the teacher. The student brings that letter back and lays it down, face up, in front of the line. Then he or she moves to the end of the line.
6. Each team continues this pattern, at its own pace, with one member at a time retrieving a letter and placing it at the front of the line to form the spelling word.
7. When team members decide that they have correctly spelled the word, they must all sit down in a straight line and be silent.
8. The teacher then checks the spelling. The teacher announces if the spelling is correct or not correct, and the activity proceeds as follows depending on the outcome.
9. If the teacher announces that the word is spelled correctly, all other teams have 1 minute to complete the spelling of their team's word.
10. If the teacher announces that the word is spelled incorrectly, the teams will continue to select letters as in the earlier steps until one team gets the spelling correct. Then step 9 will be repeated.
11. The first team to complete the correct spelling of the word wins that round. Second, third, and fourth place may be noted. With four teams, scoring would be 4, 3, 2, 1, with first place getting 4 points. Any team that does not complete the spelling of their word in the one-minute timeframe from the first correctly finishing team scores a 0 for that round. Those not following directions will also score a 0.
12. Repeat the procedure with the next word.

Box continues on next page

Preparation

Beforehand, prepare for the activity as follows:

1. Create one set of laminated alphabet cards (A through Z with extras of commonly used letters, such as A and E) per team. Use different colors of ink for each team to keep the letter cards sorted. Use a tray to hold each team's letter cards (tops from duplicating paper boxes are great for this).
2. Rehearse the movements for the activity: running, fast walking, skipping, side slide left, side step left, side slide right, side step right, backward walking, and so forth; also try the same activities but done in pairs with students hooked at the elbows.
3. Organize teams ahead of time.
4. Use a basketball court with existing lines (if available).
5. Have a watch with 1-minute timing capabilities.
6. Have a clipboard to keep score and take notes.

Also consider the following tips:

- Variation: Words other than those on the spelling list may be used. For example, ask a question and the team must spell the answer.
- The suggested amount of letters for each team's set of alphabet cards is as follows: 3-a, 2-b, 2-c, 1-d, 3-e, 2-f, 2-g, 1-h, 3-i, 1-j, 1-k, 2-I, 2-m, 2-n, 3-o, 2-p, 1-q, 2-r, 2-s, 2-t, 2-u, 1-v, 1-w, 1-x, 1-y, 1-z, for a total of 46 total cards per set (per team).
- Remember to use a different color of ink for each set for easy sorting.

CHAPTER 8

Common Core Standards
Navigating Text Complexity

Making content comprehensible across the curriculum for struggling students can be a daunting task.

> With the advent of Common Core Standards, reading complex text is a requirement. Students are expected to read increasingly complex texts with growing independence in order to reach college and career readiness (McLaughlin, & Overturf, 2013). The format of the textbook often plays a critical role in what, when, and how content will be covered. Some educators suggest that as much as 67 to 90% of secondary classroom instruction is centered on the text (Woodward & Elliott, 1990), thus making the textbook the key content provider.

The expectations of the CCSS call on teachers to instruct around complex text so students read closely to accomplish essential skills, such as make inferences, determine themes, and analyze development of ideas. They do so using textual evidence from a targeted complex text. Much like teachers engage students in the writing process to create optimal written products, teachers would likewise plan and conduct a series of comprehensive lessons to help students meet these rigorous reading standards. These lessons would align to specific reading standards, include a myriad of instructional strategies and formative assessments (e.g., read silently, discuss, listen to, take notes, engage in discussion with peers, write informally and formally, etc.), and center on text-dependent activities and tasks to illicit deep understanding of targeted texts.

How can we make these texts more accessible for struggling readers? We know that many of our students are currently reading below the level of what is required to meet the Common Core Standards implementation.

Students need to master critical comprehension skills to be successful with informational text, and as we teachers we must support students struggling with text complexity in our inclusive classrooms. Prior to the Common Core Standards, the National Reading Panel Report on Comprehension (1999) listed seven categories of comprehension instruction with a solid scientific base:

1. Monitoring
2. Question answering
3. Question generation
4. Summarizing

5. Knowledge of text structure
6. Use of graphic organizers
7. Cooperative learning

These categories support the following traditional comprehension skills:

- Finding the main idea
- Identifying details
- Detecting the sequence
- Drawing conclusions
- Determining cause and effect
- Comparing and contrasting

There is an important distinction between instructional strategies and reading strategies:

> *Instructional strategies* are activities, techniques, approaches, and methods that teachers use to promote student learning and achievement.
>
> *Reading strategies* are conscious, flexible plans learners use to make sense of what they're reading and learning; they are thinking processes that reside in the learner's head.

A further distinction to note is that there are two types of reading strategies: cognitive and metacognitive. The distinction between these two processes is very important in helping students to develop higher-level comprehension and thinking skills. Cognitive strategies are the more straightforward of the two. These are techniques that good readers use to make sense of text. Metacognitive strategies require the reader to connect with the text at a higher level—thinking more deeply about the reading and the meaning of the text. Metacognitive strategies encourage the students to "think about their thinking" and to be able to verbalize their thoughts or record their connections to text in writing.

Both cognitive and metacognitive strategies are necessary for learners to increase comprehension of and connection to text. It is essential to model effective reader strategies of both types with your students, and to do so often.

The following lists note which reading strategies are considered cognitive and which are considered metacognitive:

Cognitive

- Rereading
- Highlighting
- Reading aloud
- Taking notes
- Mapping information
- Talking to someone
- Finding key vocabulary
- Using mnemonics or other memory-enhancing techniques

Metacognitive

- Predicting
- Inferring
- Self-questioning
- Monitoring
- Clarifying
- Evaluating
- Summarizing
- Synthesizing

When teaching these strategies, we need to help students understand:

Declarative knowledge—the "what"
Procedural knowledge—the "how"
Conditional knowledge—the "why" and "when"

(Lipson & Wixson, 2003)

To help students understand these three types of knowledge—declarative, procedural, and conditional—we need to "unpack" the curriculum into digestible chunks so that students grasp both the *content* and the *process* of the lesson. Another way to describe this full picture of learning is by applying the *what, how, why,* and *when* framework to lesson planning. The "what" of teaching/learning is the **content** of the lesson. The "how" of teaching/learning is the **process** that you are asking the students to engage in—the form of both the input and the output of information. The "why" of the lesson is the **importance of the topic**. You need to teach with the end in mind. Whys are you teaching this, and why is it important for the students to learn? "The when" of teaching/learning involves the timeline required. How much time do the students have for completion of the lesson material? This involves backward planning and is an important consideration for struggling students.

Strategic reading of informational text needs to involve explicit teaching to be most effective. Note the following considerations:

- Reading instruction should focus on one strategy at a time, and eventually students should see how all of the strategies work together.
- Students should learn what, when, and how skills/strategies are used during reading.
- Teachers should model skills and strategy use with think-alouds and demonstrations.
- Instruction should be carefully scaffolded.
- The purpose for reading should include both content and the strategy focus.
- The "wrap-up" should include a review of the focus strategy, with discussion about its application in other texts. (Duffy-Hester, 2002)

TEXTBOOK PREVIEW IDEAS

The textbook previewing strategies highlighted here give teachers options for whole-class and small-group activities. By participating in these activities, students will become familiar with the organization, content, special features, and benefits of their textbooks.

Textbook Sales Pitches/Commercials

Divide the class in half. Distribute texts to the students of one group. They are going to play the part of textbook sales representatives. Allow these students time to peruse the text and get an understanding of its organization, special features, benefits, and weaknesses. Then, they will need to work together to prepare a persuasive sales pitch.

Distribute the same texts to the second group. They are to pretend that they are faculty and student members of a textbook adoption committee. They are to prepare a list of questions and concerns based on their own review of the text, considering the same features as noted for the first group.

After ample discussion time, bring the groups together and facilitate a whole-class discussion time as needed. During the whole-class discussion, the teacher evaluates the groups based on a rubric that determines the level of persuasiveness of each team. This role-playing strategy is helpful to get the students better connected to a text and to help them understand what text features are useful to the learner. The teacher can precede or follow this activity with a discussion of "considerate" versus "inconsiderate" texts, with entertaining examples.

What's Old and What's New

Break the class into small groups. Give each group a textbook chapter to review. Ask them to review the topics and special features of the chapter. Give each group a sheet of chart paper. They are to make two columns: what is old (already covered in class) and what is new (new information). Have each group share with others the old and the new information. This will be displayed on chart paper posted in the classroom and the students can take a "gallery walk" to view highlights. Recall from the previous chapter that a gallery walk is an interactive strategy in which small groups move around the classroom together to view the work of the other groups, and it's great for your kinesthetic learners. It is fast-paced, involves movement, and the discussion does not get bogged down with repetitive information.

Name That Feature

Distribute texts to students. They are to review the text and make a list of the features that they notice, define them and give examples, and state why they are important. Features in texts include the table of contents, index, highlighted vocabulary, text boxes, illustrations, headings, glossaries, and so forth. Students then compare lists. Collect the lists of features and descriptions. In another class period, play "name that feature." The teacher gives a student-generated definition of a particular feature and the students work in teams to guess the name of the feature. The team with the quickest response gets a point.

Textbook Timeline

Develop a timeline for the school year. For each month, identify the themes, units, or chapters that will be studied. Divide students into groups according to their birth months. Assign each group the section of text that will be studied that month. Each group then prepares a text tour preview for the rest of the class by creating a visual representation of the text using graphic images, concept maps, pictorial images, or other graphic techniques. Throughout the year, revisit the visual representations. with students adding to the charts after the completion of each section.

Textbook Scavenger Hunts

Provide the students with a list of items and features to find in their textbooks. They can work as individuals or small groups. Some examples include the following:

- In what appendix would you find an explanation _____ of [selected topic]?
- On what page would you find a photograph of [selected item]?
- What are the titles of the four authors contributing to the textbook?
- Each chapter ends with a summary and what other feature?

Conclude the activity with a discussion of the items.

Textbook Picture Walks

Ask students to carefully peruse the index of the textbook, noting the various themes and topics. Present students with copies of pictures or graphics from the text. Ask the students to predict which pictures might match an index heading. Have them share their predictions in small groups. Conclude with a class discussion. This will provide insights as to the students' background knowledge of the selected topics.

Sticky-Note Votes

Have students leaf through the book and place sticky notes on any feature they think is special. Bring students back together and discuss the text features they selected. Place students in small groups and have them consider their choices and create a group list of features in order of perceived importance. Moderate a discussion as each small group shares its rankings.

Fascinating Facts

Distribute textbooks and give students time to look through them. Pass out index cards and have students put their names on them. Ask students to find an artist, title, topic, picture, fact, or other item that appeals to them. Have each student note his or her choice on the index card, along with the page number where the item appears and an explanation of why it is appealing or interesting. Have students share their "fascinating facts" with the rest of the class.

Think-Aloud Summaries

In this strategy used while reading a text with the class, the teacher models through a think-aloud how to summarize, as follows:

1. Model how to generate predictions about the topic and a purpose for reading through a brief survey of the text.
2. Read the text aloud, stopping periodically to briefly summarize: "So far, this is about. . . ."
3. After modeling summarization, provide wait time for students to think of their own summary statements before you give yours.
4. At the end of the text, give an overall summary and whether your predictions were accueate or not. Have students summarize key ideas from text with a learning partner. (Zwiers, 2004)

Into, Through, and Beyond Strategies

Developing strategic reading skills is a complex process. In order for this framework for teaching comprehension to be meaningful, the teacher needs to set the stage for teaching and learning before students even open a book. It is also important to engage them in the meaning-making process throughout and during reading as well. These processes are also supported by the Common Core Standards. After the reading occurs is a time for reflection and making connections. Meaning is something that is actively created instead of passively received (Vaughn & Estes, 1986).

Figure 8.1. Into–Through–Beyond Chart

INTO	THROUGH	BEYOND
Activities to activate prior knowledge and set the stage for comprehension	*Activities to boost comprehension*	*Activities to provide for reflection and connecting learning to new experiences*
• K-W-L	• Paired Reading	• Learning Logs
• Tapping Prior Knowledge Through Questioning	• Teacher Read-Alouds	• Line-Ups
• Brainstorming	• Graphic Organizers	• Text Posters
• Quick Writes	• Partner Share	• Gallery Walk
• Teacher Read-Alouds	• Reading Journals	• Reflective Writing
• Videos	• Reader's Theatre	• Comparison to Other Works
• Text Tour	• Dramatization	• Letter to the Author
• Mapping	• Dialogue	• Rewrite Ending
• Picture or Word Prediction	• Story Board	• Debate/Panel Discussion
• Posing Problems	• Student-Generated Questions	• Small-Group/Whole-Class Discussion
• Focus Question ("Have you ever . . ." "What if . . .")	• Prediction	• Team Poster
• Anticipation Guide	• Paraphrase	• Comparison/Contrast (Venn Diagram)

This chapter provides you with a framework for teaching comprehension skills to struggling students as well as tips for integrating these strategies into your lessons to align your instruction with the Common Core Standards. The factors to consider in designing your lessons include activating prior knowledge, tuning in to various learning styles, creating a "need to know," and maintaining engagement throughout the lesson. The key shifts with the Common Core Standards involve students engaging students in close reading, increasing text complexity and focusing in on academic vocabulary. Therefore, each phase of the comprehension process— into, through, and beyond—is a vital component necessary for successful readers, especially with the emphasis on informational texts. Figure 8.1 provides examples of strategies for each phase.

RECIPROCAL TEACHING TO REINFORCE COMMON CORE STANDARDS

Overview

Reciprocal teaching (Palinscar & Brown, 1986) is a research-validated intervention designed to assist less capable readers in developing powerful reading comprehension strategies as they gain more control over their reading. It is based on structured dialogue in which the teacher begins by being the leader—modeling the strategies, guiding student responses, taking care to "think aloud" during modeling, and so on. Gradually, the teacher fades out direct instruction, turning more and more control over to the students—playing the role of coach.

Step 1: Introduce the Four Strategies

Model the reciprocal strategies after reading small segments of the text by thinking aloud.

1. Predict
   - This provides a purpose for reading—to confirm or adjust their predictions, linking prior knowledge and text information.
   - Model how to use clues from the text to support predictions— review the title, several illustrations, and text features such as the table of contents and chapter headings.
   - Share with the students what predictions are, why we use them, and what makes a good one.
2. Question
   - To generate questions, students first have to identify significant information. This information is then formed into questions as a type of self-test or to ask each other.
   - Model how to ask questions throughout the reading. Ask questions before reading as you preview the text and model the "I wonder" strategy. Pause and ask questions that require the reader to check for comprehension. Model how to answer your questions as you continue to read.
   - Provide lots of practice on how to phrase questions and why they are so helpful to reading.

Box continues on next page

- Promote the use of Bloom's taxonomy to promote higher- level questions beyond the literal knowledge level.
- Students may mark the place in the text where they have a question with a sticky note as they read to share later with the group or a partner.

3. Clarify
   - Focus students' attention on the different reasons why text may be difficult to understand, such as new vocabulary and unfamiliar or complex concepts.
   - Model clarifications during reading by using the think-aloud strategy.
     - ➤ Share with your students how to phrase clarifications.
     - ➤ Select a multisyllabic or tricky word that requires clarifying. Pause and think aloud, listing the possible word-solving strategies you could use, such as meaning in context, familiar chunks, and affixes.
     - ➤ Choose a sentence or section where the idea or concept may be puzzling and requires clarification; think aloud as you reread, noting clues the author has placed in the text to assist in clarifying meaning.
   - Stress to your students why clarifications are helpful in the reading process.

4. Summarize
   - In this step, students identify, paraphrase, and integrate important information in the text.
   - Stress to the students the importance of summarizing what they read.
   - Model the strategy by summarizing the section or page you have read aloud. Demonstrate how reading aloud several times enables you to identify key information or concepts.
   - Students should record their summaries in a concise format of 6 to 10 words or two to three sentences.
   - You may model how to underline key words or record them on sticky notes to assist with a written summary. An overhead transparency is useful for circling key words or underlining key phrases.
   - Model for the students how to paraphrase the information read in their own words.
   - Have students use a transparency in the same way in their copies of the text and use these key words to form an oral summary.
   - You could say: "I am going to round up the main idea. First I will reread the passage to myself so the information is fresh in my head, then I will be able to sum up the main idea."
   - As you reread, verbalize each of the main points as you come across them and model the construction of a summary. Have students skim and scan the same passage and then come up with an oral summary with a partner. They may use the main points you modeled.
   - Stress again how summarizing helps with reading comprehension and retention.
   - At the end of the lesson, reflect on how each of these strategies helps in understanding the reading.

Step 2: Assign Reading

Have students read a text for a brief time (10–20 minutes), depending on the ages and ability levels of your students.

Step 3: Model and Lead the Discussion

Model how to summarize the reading assignment. Paraphrase the main idea(s), important details, text structure, patterns, and so forth—be sure to think aloud. In other words, explain your thinking, the "how" and "why" of each step—for example, "Let me think, the main idea seemed to be about the way political events happen in cycles because both the title and the introduction really stressed this idea. . . ." Ask text-dependent questions to get the students connected with the text and speaking and listening to each others' responses.

Then *model self-questioning*—for example, "What was the problem here? Was there any solution? I am not sure about this idea. . . ."

Then *clarify ambiguities*—for example, "What did the author mean by _____? What does the word on page _____ mean? I'm confused about. . . ."

Finally, *predict the upcoming section*—for example, "I think the next section will explain how this election is part of another cycle because. . . ."

Step 4: Shift Control to the Students for Ongoing Practice

The key to success with reciprocal teaching is to gradually guide the students to lead the discussions of using the four strategies, explaining their thinking, arguing for their views, clarifying ambiguities, and so forth.

Informational Text Adaptations

1. Predict
    *   Brainstorm: What do we know about the topic?
    *   Predict what information might be included: "We will learn. . . because. . . ." Model how to find clues that lead to the prediction— table of contents, headings, subheadings, text conventions, and other features.
    *   Have students record their predictions on sticky notes; student pairs the place their sticky notes on a chart with headings such as the following: I think . . . I bet . . . I wonder . . . I predict . . .
    *   Prompt their predictions with questions like the following: What do you think the next section will be about? What information might be included?
2. Question
    *   Present a question word as a prompt for the students to create questions based on the text: Who? What? Where? Why? When? How?
    *   Model generating a question that is answered in the text, one that requires text information along with an inference; use the QAR sentence starters (described later in the chapter).
    *   Make cards with question words—turn the cards over; students choose one.
    *   Take turns asking and answering questions:
        *   ➢ I'm curious about . . .
        *   ➢ I wonder . . .
        *   ➢ Who? What? When? Why?
        *   ➢ One question I had about what I read was . . .
        *   ➢ What were you thinking about as you were reading?

Box continues on next page

➢ What is a question that you could ask about this page (section)? What is the answer? How did you get that answer? (This is a form of self-test.)

➢ What questions would a teacher ask? (Have students generate answers.)

3. Clarify
   - Focus attention on the reasons why text is difficult to understand—roadblocks to understanding mean that students need to reread, read ahead, or seek assistance
   - Identify a difficult or unfamiliar word or concept, and model how to clarify it (focus on one word/concept at each session): "How can I figure out that word?" Then model the use of fix-up strategies:
     ➢ Reread the sentence—key ideas? Think about what I know.
     ➢ Reread sentences before/after to look for clues.
     ➢ Break the word apart; look for parts I know.
     ➢ Think of a word that looks like this one.
     ➢ Look for prefix, suffix.
     ➢ Try another word that makes sense.
   - Question students after reading:
     ➢ Are there any words you thought were interesting or puzzling?
     ➢ How did you figure out a puzzling word? Give two ways.
     ➢ Were there any parts that were hard to understand?
     ➢ What did the authors mean when they said. . .?
     ➢ What does the word _____ mean? This is a tricky word because. . .
   - Have students share their strategies and points:
     ➢ This is confusing to me. I need to. . .(e.g., reread)
     ➢ What I'm thinking is. . ., but that doesn't make sense. I need to. . .
     ➢ One of the words I wasn't sure about was. . .
     ➢ What other words do I know that I can use in place of. . .?
     ➢ This sentence/page is not clear. I need to. . .

4. Summarize

   This strategy provides the opportunity to identify and integrate important information from the text. Model this technique by recording student suggestions on the white board. Use sentence starters and cloze sentence frames to begin, then follow these steps:
   - Discuss text points and decide which ones belong in the summary.
   - Have students restate main ideas in their own words (10 words or less).
   - Share responses as a class:
     ➢ What is the most important person, place, or thing?
     ➢ What does the author want us to remember or learn from this passage?
     ➢ Use a sequence to organize main ideas: First . . . Next . . . Then . . . Finally . . .

Use these prompts to get started with Reciprocal Teaching and modeling the process with the students. See Figure 8.2.

Figure 8.2. Conversation Cards: Reciprocal Teaching

1. Predict	2. Question:
• Let's look at the book's cover. What do you think we will be reading about? • Look through the illustrations. How do the pictures add to the meaning of the text? • Use clues from the illustrations and your own knowledge to make a prediction. • How will you explain why you made this prediction? • Our predictions are: • The clues we used were:	*Before Reading:* • Think of some questions you can ask as you read the book. *After Reading:* • One question I had about what I read was . . . • What did you think about as you were reading? • Reread the text and make some questions to ask. • Ask questions that begin with *who, what, where, when, why, how,* or *what if.* • Ask a question that you can't answer directly from the text. What clues in the text and your own experiences did you use in the question and answer? • Ask questions that are based on the big ideas and some details of the reading. Our questions are:
3. Clarifying	**4. Summarize:**

• Think about parts that are confusing to you.
• Reread, looking for words or ideas that you do not understand.
• List one or two puzzling words/ideas.
• What strategy did you use for confusing or puzzling words/ideas?
• Reread. Find chunks you know. Check it. Reread. Does it make sense now?
 	
A difficult word/idea we found is: _____
We figured out the word/idea by:
	• Skim the text and pictures to find main ideas.
	• Summarize the ideas in your own words.
	  ➢ Share the important events in order.
	  ➢ In nonfiction, use words such as: **first, next, then, finally.**
	  ➢ In fiction, use words such as: *setting, characters, problem, events, ending.*
	
	Our summary:

Duplicate conversation cards for student questions on cardstock. Students work in reciprocal teaching teams as they predict, question, clarify and summarize. See Figure 8.3

Figure 8.3. Student Comprehension Cards

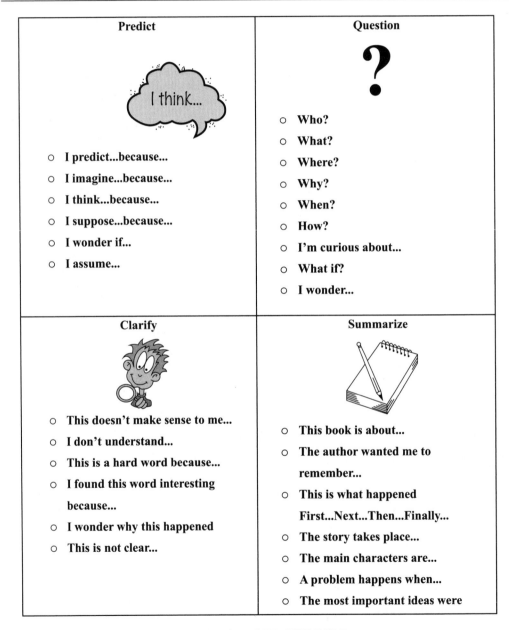

Predict	Question
I think... o I predict...because... o I imagine...because... o I think...because... o I suppose...because... o I wonder if... o I assume...	? o Who? o What? o Where? o Why? o When? o How? o I'm curious about... o What if? o I wonder...
Clarify o This doesn't make sense to me... o I don't understand... o This is a hard word because... o I found this word interesting because... o I wonder why this happened o This is not clear...	**Summarize** o This book is about... o The author wanted me to remember... o This is what happened First...Next...Then...Finally... o The story takes place... o The main characters are... o A problem happens when... o The most important ideas were

ELABORATION AND EXTENSION STRATEGIES

Overview

There are many techniques that can be used to extend and elaborate the connection with text, background knowledge, and comprehension. Such strategies have the following features:

- They are appropriate across all curriculum areas.
- They are used *during* reading and are also important to use *after* reading.
- They build connections between the students' background knowledge and the text.
- They can assist and support struggling readers through the use of visual and auditory input.

What Are Elaboration and Extension Strategies?

These techniques help struggling students make connections with text and enhance background knowledge. This additional processing of the text and/or the visual/auditory experiences often results in increased comprehension. The process involves generating questions, making inferences, and evaluating the information. The rationale for using these strategies is that the more students interact with the text, the better they will understand it.

GENERATING QUESTIONS

"Readers understand that hearing other's questions inspires new ones of their own; likewise, listening to other's answers can also inspire new thinking" (Miller, 2005).

Overview

Effective readers generate their own questions as they read. This sets a purpose for reading and develops motivation to seek answers to those questions. It is important that students know what to ask and how to ask for it. Brainstorm with students under these headings:

- How does asking questions help the reader?
- Why do readers ask questions?
- How do readers figure out the answers to their questions?

Implementation

Use the following steps to implement the questioning web strategy:

- Define the process of generating questions.
- Model the process of generating questions.
- Together, generate a list of questions from the reading.
- Then select a question from the list: "Let's choose a question from our list, one that we really want to figure out, and think out loud about how we might make sense of it."
- The question is written in the center of the web and possible answers are recorded on the web lines (see Figure 8.4). The answer the students finally arrive at is recorded at the bottom.
- Talk about all the different ways students thought about or interpreted the question.

Figure 8.4. Questioning Web

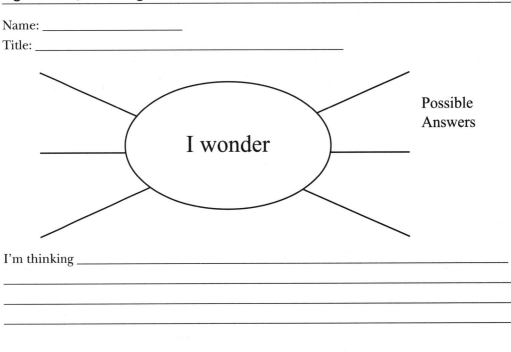

Name: _____

Title: _____

I'm thinking _____

_____

_____

_____

MAKING INFERENCES

Overview

Inferential thinking for struggling readers can be a difficult process. It involves going beyond the facts and details and "reading between the lines." Most reading experts, such as P. David Pearson (1981), agree that instruction in inferential thinking while reading should begin early and should be modeled and constantly reinforced.

Implementation

Use the following steps to implement this strategy:

1. Define and explain inferences to your students. Stress to the students that readers must put together clues and go beyond the words written on the page.
2. Model the process of generating inferences. Sharing excerpts from a book or video and pausing to do think-aloud strategies would help in this process.
3. Work with the students on a common piece of text. It is important to select suitable material (either narrative or informational text) that provides students with opportunities to draw conclusions. Students need to realize that these ideas are not boldly stated in text and that they need to draw conclusions based on the text and their personal experiences.
4. Provide guided student practice in making inferences from the selected text. Ask students to read a common selection you have chosen and then present them with a series of inferential questions. It is helpful to have students work in pairs to create their own inferential questions.

PREDICTING AND QUESTIONING WITH NONFICTION TEXT

Overview

Informational texts can be particularly daunting for struggling readers. Narrative texts are much more accessible to them. Therefore, following a carefully designed sequence of techniques, prompts, predictions, and questions will assist and support students' comprehension of nonfiction text.

Implementation

When introducing the book, try the following prompts and strategies that are carefully sequenced to help your struggling readers succeed:

Nonfiction Text Features

- What do you notice about nonfiction? How is it different from fiction? What is the purpose of nonfiction text? What are the different kinds of nonfiction text? Which nonfiction texts you do you like to read?
- Students may look quickly through the book and record the features they noticed on a "What We Know About Nonfiction" chart, or a two-column chart with the headings of Conventions/Purpose.

Title

- Brainstorm and list words that might be in the book.
- Ask questions using these words.

Table of Contents

- Will our questions be answered? Where?
- Generate further questions from the table of contents.

Chapters

- Read a sentence from a chapter, noting "I won't tell you which chapter this sentence is from."
- Students predict which chapter it came from and check chapters to confirm.

Text Features

- Review examples of how information is presented in a nonfiction text: sketches, maps, diagrams, photos, captions, labels, connected text. Ask, "How do these help you to predict?" Review each feature separately and discuss its contribution to understanding the information.
- Describe an illustration or graphic from the book, but do not show it to the students.
- Ask, "Which chapter might it come from?" Students predict which chapter it came from and check chapters to confirm.

Box continues on next page

What I Know, What I Wonder

- Have students record one thing they know (green) and one thing they wonder (yellow) on sticky notes or sentence strips and display these as a guide for the reading.

Reading the Text

- Establish the purpose for reading: Students read to find out specific information to add to a graphic organizer and/or find answers to their questions.
- Students silently read the text. The teacher may coach with prompts.
- Students place sticky notes in the text or record the following on index cards (these may be color-coded notes/cards):
  - ➤ Questions they will ask the other students or the teacher
  - ➤ Questions they have about a specific point or section
  - ➤ An interesting detail, new information, surprising information, or something they already knew
  - ➤ A difficult or interesting word
  - ➤ Connections from text to self (TS), text to text (TT), or text to world (TW)
- Questions may be organized into four categories:
  - ➤ Fact: Who? What? Where? When? How?
  - ➤ Inquiry: Why? Do you think. . .? What if. . .?
  - ➤ Vocabulary: What does _____ mean?
  - ➤ Experience: Have you ever . . . .?
- At the end of each chapter or section, instruct students to reflect on what they have learned so far and what they expect to learn next. They should review the content and how it is organized. Have them skim the subtitles of the next chapter and study the illustrations and captions to make further predictions.

Returning to the Text

- Prompt students to reflect on the strategies that were used to understand nonfiction text:
  - ➤ What features of the text helped you understand it?
  - ➤ How did you use the headings, illustrations, diagrams, and table of contents to help you read the text?
  - ➤ How did you figure out the hard words?
  - ➤ Did you reread parts that were confusing, difficult, or important?
  - ➤ What questions did you have before, during, and after reading? How were those questions answered? Do you still wonder about some questions?
- Summarize the strategies by making a chart of students' responses: "When I read nonfiction, I. . . ."
- Have students check their predictions/questions and add information to their KWL charts.

- As a class, share reactions to the book: "What did you think about. . .?" or "Did you like the ending?"
- Build a graphic organizer to reflect upon the content. Have students write or draw on the chart (list headings, diagrams, etc.).
- As a class, construct a "Book of Nonfiction Conventions," with an example on each page.

USING VISUAL IMAGES

Overview

Frequently when we read, our brains create pictures of what we read and what the text describes—it is like creating a movie in our minds. This process is called *imaging*. Struggling readers often lack background knowledge of what they read; therefore, their pictures may be incomplete or inaccurate. Students' visual imaging can help a teacher determine where they may be having confusion in their reading comprehension or lack background knowledge.

Implementation

Use the following steps to implement this strategy:

1. Define the process of visual imaging. Explain that creating visual images helps the reader make meaning, helps the reader retain information from the text, and promotes comprehension. These visual images may differ from student to student.
2. Model the process of using visual images. Select a portion of vivid text that lends itself to "picture making" and do a teacher read-aloud of the passage. Draw a quick picture on the overhead or board of the images evoked from this passage. Ask the students how their visual images might differ.
3. Provide direct instruction in visual imagery and the importance of visual literacy. Select a portion of informational or narrative text to read aloud, pausing frequently to ask the students what pictures are in their minds. Have students share their impressions. After the passage is complete, have the students do a quick sketch of the images or graphic symbols that represent what they found memorable. Have students share with their learning partners. Discuss how all of the images differ because we all perceive ideas based on our personal background experience.
4. Allow students to practice visual images on their own. Select a portion of text or a story that the students will interact with and have them follow the previous process of creating visual imagery. Students then share their images with partners and the whole class.

QUESTION–ANSWER RELATIONSHIP (QAR) STRATEGY

Overview

The question–answer relationship, or QAR, strategy (Raphael, 1996) is a thinking strategy that helps students answer comprehension questions more efficiently by analyzing the task demands of various types of questions. Students learn to categorize comprehension questions according to where they might find the answers to these questions.

> QAR is a student-centered approach to questioning because it "clarifies how students can approach the task of reading texts and answering questions" (Raphael, 1986, p. 517). This is a helpful tool for teachers to develop questions and serves as a strategy for students in answering questions.

Preparation

Model to the students the four levels of questioning associated with text (Figure 8.5). Provide lots of examples using think-aloud strategies. Make sure that they understand these levels before having them proceed on their own.

Figure 8.5. Question–Answer Relationships Focus on Four Types of Questions

In the Book QARs	In My Head QARs
Right There	*Author and You*
This answer is in the text, and is usually easy to find. The words used to make up the question and the words used to answer the question are "right there." These are questions/answers stated in the text.	This answer in not in the story or the text directly. You need to think about what you already know, what the author tells you in the text, and how it fits together.
Think and Search (Putting It Together)	*On My Own*
This answer is in the story or text but you need to put together different facts or parts of the story to find it. The words for the question and the words for the answer are not found in the same sentence. They come from different parts of the text.	This is a higher-level question. The answer will not be in the story or the text. You can sometimes even answer the question without reading the story. This answer comes from your own experiences and background.

Additional Suggestions

For struggling students, you can combine the four levels of questioning to three and provide a picture icon to represent the type of question being asked, as in the following examples. You could make cards from these examples and provide them to the students for better understanding of the meaning of the various levels.

Examples of questions at each level

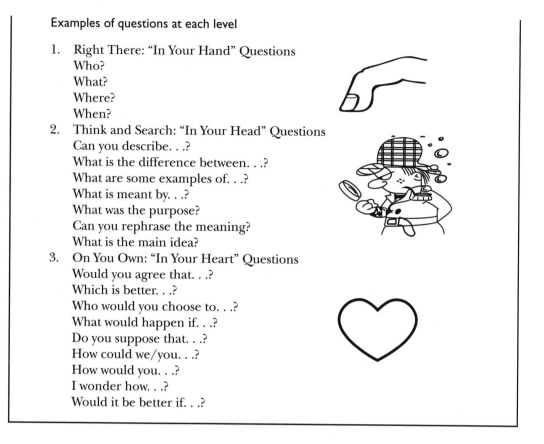

1. Right There: "In Your Hand" Questions
    Who?
    What?
    Where?
    When?
2. Think and Search: "In Your Head" Questions
    Can you describe. . .?
    What is the difference between. . .?
    What are some examples of. . .?
    What is meant by. . .?
    What was the purpose?
    Can you rephrase the meaning?
    What is the main idea?
3. On You Own: "In Your Heart" Questions
    Would you agree that. . .?
    Which is better. . .?
    Who would you choose to. . .?
    What would happen if. . .?
    Do you suppose that. . .?
    How could we/you. . .?
    How would you. . .?
    I wonder how. . .?
    Would it be better if. . .?

QAR FOR OLDER STUDENTS

The QAR strategy can also be used with older students. Model the procedure for answering questions, and note the following steps for students:

1. Read the question before reading the text. This helps you know what to look for. It engages the brain and increases awareness of details that may be helpful later.
2. Questions can be easy to answer with a few words or phrases from the text, or a bit more challenging if an answer is implied in the reading or composed of details from different parts of the text. Some questions ask for opinions or connections to the reader's life.
3. Think about the levels of questioning and determine the level of the question you are trying to answer.

Teacher tips for implementation of this strategy include the following:

*   Practice this strategy with short paragraphs before reading longer text and answering related questions. Use a variety of texts, fictional and informational.

Box continues on next page

- Color code the questions you present for students to answer to reinforce their recognition of the different types of questions and answers. Use a picture of a traffic signal with a green, yellow, and red light.

  ➤ Green light questions are the simplest kind of question to answer. The answers to these questions will be "right there" in the text (literal).

  ➤ Yellow light questions require "think and search." To construct and answer, you need to slow down and look in more than one place in the text. The answer words are there in the text, but they are in several locations and may be more implicit than directly stated. Example questions: "In what three ways are _____ like _____?" or "How do you know that _____ caused that?"

  ➤ Red light questions require you to stop and to think about what the passage means (textual information) and what you already know (prior knowledge) about the topic. You develop the answer on your own, using the text for support. These questions require you to demonstrate your understanding of what you have read, and elaborate upon it using your own personal experiences.

DOUBLE-ENTRY JOURNALS

Overview

Double-entry journals (Harvey & Goudvis, 2000) are a responding strategy appropriate for all content areas and grade levels. A double-entry journal consists of a two-part log in which the student responds to self-selected or teacher-selected portions of a text or story. This response strategy links the reading–writing–thinking connection by having students express their thoughts, feelings, and ideas about a text. Students look for an aspect of the text or story that they find interesting and respond to the information; this could be a statement, quote, idea, thought or event. In their journals, they record their thoughts and reactions to the selection. Double-entry journals are like having a "conversation with the author."

The purpose of a double-entry journal is to not just have students paraphrase what is in the text or story, but to go deeper and make personal connections. This strategy helps them reflect as readers and utilizes their critical thinking skills.

Implementation

Students take a sheet of paper and fold it in half lengthwise. One side says "Note-taking" and the other side says "Note-making." Students are asked to take their notes on one side and actively respond on the other. Their responses might range from agree or disagree, to questions, clarifications, or personal thoughts. For example, you might ask the students to select four significant quotes from the chapter or text. After writing their quotes on the "Note-taking" side, they provide a personalized response on the "Note-making" side—for example, "I liked this quote because . . ." or "This quote reminds me of . . . ."

The steps to implement this strategy are as follows:

1. Select the text or story you will use to model the strategy.
2. Read the selection to the students.
3. Introduce the double-entry format by folding a sheet of paper in half and adding the "Note-taking" and "Note-making" headings.
4. Select portions of text to react to (prompts are shown in Figure 8.6).
5. Model how to take notes on the "Note-taking" side of the journal as you read.
6. After reading, model how to write responses on the "Note-making" side.
7. Ask the students for additional responses that they would like to add.
8. Assign students a section of informational or narrative text to respond to, and have them follow the modeled steps to create double-entry journals. Note that the journals are completed before, after, and during reading.
9. Provide time for students to share their double-entry journals with learning partners.

Figure 8.6. Format and Prompts for Double-Entry Journals

Words from Text	Important Ideas/Information	
What's Interesting	What's Important	
Facts	Questions	Responses

Figure 8.7. Text-Dependent Questions Graphic Organizer

Directions: After rereading the text, write answers to questions in the "My Response" section. Support each response by recording textual evidence in the "Evidence from the Text" section. After you are given time to talk to a classmate and share ideas, complete the "My Thoughts Now" section based on your conversation.

1 . QUESTION	
My Response	**Evidence From the Text**
My Thoughts Now	

COMMON EXPOSITORY TEXT STRUCTURES

In order to support students who might find informational books challenging, it is important to explicitly teach certain basic text structures. Provide them with samples of each text structure. Discuss how they are different, noting distinct features. Make sure they pay attention to the signal words that give them clues as to what type of text structure they are reading. The following list provides descriptions of text structures, their signal words, and appropriate graphic organizers students can use to summarize the information. Knowing text structures will assist your struggling students in their content-area reading.

Description:
   Presents a topic, provides details that help readers understand the
      characteristics of a topic or idea, such as a person, place, or thing.
   Signal Words: No specific signal words
   Graphic Organizer: Web organized into categories of information

Sequence:
   Puts facts, events, or concepts in order of their occurrence. Used for giving
      directions or explaining stages in life cycle, for example.
   Signal Words: first, second, third, then, next, last, before, after, finally
   Graphic Organizer Series of events organized in boxes with arrows

Comparison and Contrast:
   Focuses on identifying similarities and differences between facts, concepts,
      people and so forth—for example, comparing crocodiles and alligators, or
      life in ancient times with today.
   Signal Words: same as, alike, similar to, resembles, compared to, different
      from, unlike, but, yet
   Graphic Organizer: Venn diagram

Cause and Effect:
   Describes causes and the resulting effects.
   Signal Words: if, so, so that, because of, as a result of, since, in order to, cause,
      effect
   Graphic Organizer Circles or squares with connecting arrows to illustrate
      relationships between causes and their effects

Problem and Solution:
   Shows the development of a problem and its solution—for example, why
      money was invented, or why you should buy a product.
   Signal Words: problem, solution, because, since, as a result, so that
   Graphic Organizer: Defining components of a problem and possible solutions
      in a two-column chart

RETELLING WITH INFORMATIONAL TEXT

Overview

Text for younger students often has a consistent structure, whereas more complex text may combine several structures. In many informational books, signal words are used. In some, they may be implicitly stated. Focus on the text layout, headings, table of contents, and other features that provide clues about the structure of the text. Some structures are easier than others. The sequence of text structures in order of difficulty is as follows: sequence, compare and contrast, description, cause and effect.

Implementation

Introducing the text structure: Introduce the text pattern or structure—the way the book is organized. Explain how and why authors use this text structure, as well as its signal words and features.

Modeling the retelling process (Moss, 2004):

1. *Read aloud* a trade book or passage, or have students read one, that illustrates a text structure. *Before reading,* link the students' experience to the text with KWL charts or brainstorming (see the problem/solution example).
2. *During the reading,* point out specific text features, such as signal words, bolded words, maps, charts, and diagrams. Ask students to listen for signal words that can help them identify the structure if these words have been previously introduced. Instruct students to listen/read carefully to remember as much about the text as they can.
3. *After reading,* retell the text as completely as possible. Ask students to complete any missing information. Model "looking back" by rereading or guiding students to reread sections that may have been missed in the retelling. You may complete the graphic organizer with student input.
4. *Embellish retellings* with analogies, personal anecdotes, and imagery so that students see how to make the text their own. Encourage students to make connections.

In later sessions: Have students predict what the text might be about and the organizational pattern by previewing the text features or table of contents. Prompt student retelling: *What did you find out first? What did you find out next? What did you learn after that?* Record responses on a chart or white board. Display illustrations to support retelling when necessary.

CODING THE TEXT: ENGAGING THE READER

Overview

The coding marking system is an active reading strategy to engage your students and facilitate their interaction with text. It is a particularly helpful way for less-skilled readers to become more aware of breakdowns in comprehension so that they can remember to clarify any issues at a later time. This is most effective when students have their own books or copies of articles and stories and can mark in them. However, students can use sticky notes, separate sheets of paper, strips of paper in the margins, and so forth to deal with common-use, nonconsumable textbooks (Perez, 2008).

Implementation

Students record their responses as they read in a journal format or using sticky notes within the text. For example, they may flag the text where they learned a new fact; use the codes to record one thing they know before reading the book based on the picture walk or preview; or, after reading/hearing the book, they may note one thing they wonder about (Harvey & Goudvis, 2000). Figure 8.8 shows common coding symbols and their meanings.

Figure 8.8. Text Coding Symbols

√	I already knew this
☆	I learned this
?	I wonder (have a question about) I liked this part and want to share it
💡	Aha! (big idea surfaces) Now I understand . . . This tells me . . .
▌	This did not make sense
!	Wow! This is amazing, exciting

CHAPTER 9

Curriculum Modification
Adapting Familiar Lessons

WHAT DO I NEED TO MODIFY?
HOW DO I ACCOMMODATE FOR DIFFERENCES?

Instructional materials and formative assessments can be adjusted to meet the individual needs of your struggling readers. There is a distinction between modifications and accommodations. In general, *accommodations* involve making the learning task more suitable by adjusting to the individual needs of the learning situation. A *modification,* on the other hand, is making the learning task different. Accommodations and modifications in the classroom are designed to be flexible and provide all students with greater access to the content being taught and the evaluation of learning that is being assessed. Students need opportunities to present and learn information in diverse ways that support their strengths and learning styles.

When you work with a classroom of students with varying entry points to learning, and with disabilities, you will need to adapt and modify the curriculum so that all students have a better chance of task completion and success. It is a challenge, if not impossible, to fit our students of different backgrounds, learning needs, and abilities into pre-packaged curriculum kits with scripted expectations.

Recent legislation has mandated the application of appropriate accommodations and modifications for struggling students in the general education classrooms. The Individuals with Disabilities Education Act of 2004 (IDEA 2004) supports accommodating the unique learning needs of students with special needs and modifying the instructional materials used in the general education classroom. This legislation provides guidelines so that students with disabilities are appropriately served in the least restrictive environment to meet their individual needs. These are essential components of effective instruction. Because IDEA specifies that students with disabilities be served in the "least restrictive environment," general education teachers need techniques to help them be successful. It is unfortunate that legal mandates need to emphasize the importance of these accommodations; the curriculum should fit the student and not the other way around.

In this chapter you will find many different accommodations and modifications to maximize the learning of all of your students. Attention has been paid to techniques that support various content areas and that support the learning styles of your diverse learners. Because you have a diversity of learners in your inclusive classroom, numerous appropriate accommodations and modifications are available for use with your students. It is the intent of this chapter to provide you with a menu of options from which to select appropriate accommodations and modifications, depending on the age and ability levels of your students. Specific strategies will be discussed that provide you with insight in meeting the unique needs of your learners. It is important that modifications and accommodations to the student's program are included in the student's individualized education plan (IEP).

MODIFICATION AND ACCOMMODATION STRATEGIES

Modification and accommodation techniques will impact the delivery of your instruction. They are designed to provide special educators and general education teachers in inclusive classrooms with multiple options. In general, *accommodation* means to make the lesson more suitable by adjusting the curriculum to meet the individual needs of the student. As stated previously, accommodations usually do not involve adjusting the material being presented to the student. The content is similar to the content being presented to other students. However, students with disabilities might require specific accommodations so that they can properly access and demonstrate understanding of the material.

A *modification,* on the other hand, is making the instruction, in content and delivery, something different. In other words, curriculum modification includes a continuum of a wide range of modified educational components. Similarly, Comfort (1990) defines curriculum modification as "the adapting or interpreting of a school's formal curriculum by teachers into learning objectives and units of learning activities judged most reasonable for an individual learner or particular group of learners" (p. 397) What follows are strategies to assist you in developing a more inclusive classroom setting. Keep in mind that these modifications should be applied on an individual basis to maximize the learning of all students. The primary purpose is to support independent growth for all students and to ensure that students with special needs are exposed to the same content as their peers.

How do you create a more inclusive classroom setting? The following tools, techniques, and strategies will assist your students as they learn, retain, and recall information presented in different ways. Some of these techniques will enhance the students' strengths and interests. For others, the techniques will help them compensate for their weaknesses, which would compromise their success in an inclusive setting.

Lesson Presentation

It all begins with careful attention to lesson preparation and design, keeping in mind that students with special needs also need the same access to content as their nondisabled peers. Choose your strategies carefully, considering each individual student's unique needs. Here are some suggestions:

- Provide an outline, key concepts list, or vocabulary list prior to the lesson.
- Pace the lesson appropriately.
- Include a variety of activities addressing various learning styles.
- Provide visual, auditory, and kinesthetic input where possible.

- Get students actively involved in the lesson: questions, partners, group work, games, and so forth.
- Provide peer-tutoring opportunities to help students review concepts.

Oral Directions

Providing clear directions is an essential step in the instructional process for students with special needs. It is preferable to provide directions to the students both verbally and visually to ensure maximum comprehension. Here are some pointers to keep in mind:

- Have students' attention before giving directions.
- Keep directions concise and simple.
- Simplify the vocabulary.
- Accompany all verbal explanations with visual demonstration when possible.
- Break down directions into one- or two-step components.
- Use peer helpers to prompt students through multistep directions.
- Have students repeat directions back to you or to peers to check understanding.
- Use a combination of visual and auditory directions. Use pictures for each step.
- Tape record daily assignments.

Written Directions

Written directions reinforce the clarity of the assignment for students with special needs. Some students have difficulty processing the information orally. Therefore, they may not understand a lecture that is being presented orally because they do not process the content in an auditory manner. These low-prep accommodations increase the opportunity for students to clearly understand the expectations of the assignment:

- Provide directions in sequential order. Place a colored dot between each step.
- Allow extra time for students to copy the assignment.
- Ask students to read the directions two or three times before asking for help.
- Always check for understanding before students begin an assignment. Have them repeat the directions or share their understanding with learning partners.

Daily Assignments

There are some simple steps to take to ensure that daily assignments are more easily understood by your students with special needs. By modifying classroom delivery of everyday assignments, you will provide greater access to instruction and daily routines.

As you prepare to look at the delivery of content, focus on the presentation of materials and consider the barriers that some students might have. Barriers might include the presentation of the material and pictures, sound material, the text content, and hands-on (kinesthetic) material. Keep the following in mind:

- Keep the page format simple. Include no extraneous pictures and provide only one to two activities per page.
- Type simple directions, underlining or bolding key words/directions.
- Create a simple border around the parts of the page you wish to emphasize.
- Give frequent short quizzes instead of one long test.
- Shorten assignments, giving just enough work to ensure mastery of skills. For example, you could break assignments into smaller segments and complete over several days.
- Allow students to work with learning partners or in cooperative groups.
- Provide study guides and/or practice take-home tests.
- Provide alternative settings for students to take tests.
- Allow students to respond orally and write the responses for the student.
- Provide extra time for completion of assignments.
- Allow students to illustrate their answers.
- Provide supplementary materials that complement the assignment at an easier reading level.
- Allow students access to a laptop or desktop computer to complete assignments.

Organization

Students with special needs often lack the ability to organize and prioritize their assignments. Teachers therefore need to make some adjustments in order for students to have greater access to the content being taught. Modifying the physical organization of the classroom can make the environment much more conducive for learning for students with special needs. It is important to provide flexible and versatile learning environments to maximize the learning for all of our students.

For instance, students who are easily distracted might benefit from the use of easily constructed study carrels made out of tri-fold poster boards. These individual "offices" help focus their attention on the work and reduce extraneous visual and auditory interference. Here are some more ideas:

- Use individual assignments sheets or charts.
- Provide student with a "Things to Do Today" pad.
- Teach students to use a daily planner or binder reminder.
- Help students to develop a system to keep track of completed work, work in progress, and corrected work (e.g., accordion file or homework folder). Tape a large manila envelope to the inside of the student's desk to store incomplete assignments.
- Develop daily routines to help students remember specific procedures.
- Color code folders for each subject.

- Post/provide due dates of assignments on a class chart or white board each day.
- Consider using a website such as schoolnotes.com to post assignments so that students and parents have access at home.
- Allow students to call home and leave a message on the home voicemail about the homework as a reminder.
- Divide long-term assignments into sections and provide due dates or time for the completion of each section.
- Outline steps in checklist form for following directions or procedures.
- Establish and post a daily classroom routine or schedule (e.g., warm-up, homework review, journal).
- Provide study guides or outlines of the content for which the student needs to be responsible.
- Provide time each week to go over organization skills as a whole class (e.g., check binder reminders and notebooks). Specifically teach these organization skills.

Behavior and Attention Difficulties

Behavior problems and attention difficulties can interfere with learning. It is important at the beginning of the year to clearly establish classroom management routines, rules, and procedures. These should also be reviewed and posted throughout the year so that all students are aware of them.

Many of your students with special needs have a history of failure over the years that they bring to your class. This reaction to school failure can manifest itself in many ways: hostility, resistance, learned helplessness, discouragement, distractibility, and withdrawal. Helping special needs students develop that "can-do" attitude will contribute to their success and confidence in your classroom. It is important to have techniques to help manage behavior so that social problems are not compounded. Careful observations and keeping anecdotal records to plan interventions are beneficial techniques. Other ideas include the following:

- Implement an individual behavior contract if needed.
- Provide a daily schedule and alert the students if there are any changes.
- Use a timer to help students stay focused for a specific period. This provides a visual and auditory reminder of the specific limits for the assignment.
- Provide "stretch" breaks after longer work sessions.
- Establish a "secret signal" to remind a student to return to task.
- Give the student choices when possible. They may choose to illustrate an idea from a core literature novel rather than write a paragraph, for example.
- Be precise about classroom procedures and routines to assist students during transition times.
- Praise specific behaviors, avoiding general and vague praise statements. Always state the positive action you would like to see: "Walk please" rather than "No running."
- Be as consistent as possible in following through on classroom and individual programs.

- Set hourly, daily, weekly, or monthly goals with an individual student as appropriate and provide frequent feedback on the student's progress.
- Partner a struggling student with a positive peer role model.
- Make positive phone calls home "just because."
- Be patient and flexible.
- Use eye contact when talking one on one with a student.
- Provide immediate feedback on performance.
- Try to limit directions to one or two steps.
- Allow ample time for hands-on instruction (actively engage students in the learning process).

Homework

What are some ideas to help your students with homework? Careful preparation is needed so that homework becomes more "family friendly" and not a burden for the student or the parents. Here are some suggestions:

- Whenever possible, shorten homework assignments (e.g., 10 math problems instead of 20).
- Go over each and every homework assignment. Check for understanding of directions.
- Give plenty of time for students to copy assignments or prepare homework agendas and have parents sign off in acknowledgment.
- At "Back to School Night," share ideas and strategies for positive homework completion with parents. Be sure to stress the importance of consistent procedures at home as well.
- Institute a homework buddy system where the buddies check each other to make sure the assignments are understood and all necessary materials are available. Have the students exchange phone numbers if appropriate.
- Set up a homework assignment sheet or daily planner/binder reminder for individual students.
- Provide study guides or vocabulary lists each week or with each unit so that students knows what will be expected.
- Ask for periodic status reports on longer assignments (e.g., book reports, research papers).
- Provide a sequential list of tasks when giving a student an independent assignment.

Textbook Modifications

Reading textbooks can be a daunting task for struggling students. The content, format, and process of reading a textbook require very distinct strategies than those for reading a narrative story. When students have comprehension problems, the task of text instruction becomes much more complex. What are some strategies that teachers can use to help students learn from informational text if they have difficulty understanding the content?

These problems are of particular concern for secondary teachers. They do not always feel that they have the skills to teach the content and to teach reading skills.

Depending on the student differences and special needs in your classroom, these strategies can be used independently, in partners, and in small groups. Students often increase their comprehension with the peer support of learning partners. The variety of techniques provided in the following lists will tune in to students' varying learning styles and will foster individual success.

Preview or **Preteach** Materials in Advance

- Provide the option to listen to a recording of the material before it is read in class.
- Preview and discuss pictures in textbooks before the material is read in class.
- Review boldfaced words from the text with the students.
- Provide students with a list of discussion questions before they read the text.
- Highlight important information in a student's textbook or color code the textbook.
- Have students look at pictures, charts, and boldface headings and construct questions about them. This will assist in reading with a purpose.

On-the-Spot Textbook Modifications

- Read text aloud, stopping frequently to ask questions, summarize, and paraphrase.
- When asked to read aloud, allow the student to pass or read to a partner instead.
- Provide an outline and allow student to takes notes while others read aloud.
- Provide supplemental materials featuring high-interest, low-vocabulary text.
- Record a read-aloud text or story for reinforcement at a later time.
- Have students read with learning partners. They each take turns reading only as much as one hand can cover. This "chunking" technique will help the struggling students better comprehend the material. After they read, they paraphrase in their own words what they found memorable with the passage.
- The "Sketch-to-Stretch" technique (Hoyt, 1999) is an excellent tool to boost visual literacy and reinforce comprehension. Have the students work with learning partners and read as much as one hand can cover to chunk the information. This time, they do a quick sketch of what they found memorable. This sketch can be a symbol, a graphic image, or any other visual representation.

Tracking Difficulties (Ability to Follow Print on Page With a Left-to-Right Progression; Requires Proper Eye-Sweep Technique)

- Partner a struggling student with a peer and allow the peer to assist with visual tracking.
- Give oral location clues when reading aloud.

- Place a horizontal arrow running from the left side to the right side of an index card to assist with directionality.
- Cut a window in an index card to assist with focusing on one line of text.
- Provide a picture frame made from construction paper.
- Allow students to listen to material and look at pictures while someone else reads aloud.

Sensory Modifications

Students with specific sensory impairments can benefit from basic adaptations of the content and process of instruction in order for them to access the material more successfully. The following lists note ideas for specific impairments.

Hearing Impairments

- The student should be seated near the teacher.
- Make a "phonics phone" out of PVC pipe (as described in an earlier chapter) from your hardware store. A student with auditory discrimination problems can subvocalize words into the phonics phone and they are understood more clearly as they travel directly from the student's mouth to the ears.
- Use visual signals frequently to secure the student's attention.
- Rephrase the content-area material when reviewing lectures.
- Provide outlines and vocabulary words in written format before introducing new material.
- Present new vocabulary in sentences instead of in isolation.
- If the student reads lips, a swivel chair is beneficial.

Vision Impairments

- Provide text in enlarged print or Braille.
- Provide magnifiers for enlarging text.
- Use computer software with enlarged fonts and pictures.
- Provide material on CDs.
- Allow extra time to complete assignments.
- When asking a question, address the student by name.
- Tape record daily assignments.
- Provide hands-on experiences whenever possible.

MODIFICATIONS IN SPECIFIC CONTENT AREAS

In addition to the general modifications described earlier in this chapter, it is important to pay particular attention to specific content areas and the unique demands that these require. Although these considerations have been effective in many different classroom settings, please be flexible in adapting them to meet the needs of your individual learners.

WRITTEN LANGUAGE MODIFICATIONS

Journals:

- Free response: the student chooses and writes freely about a topic.
- Use a question-and-answer format.
- Sequence cards: the student places the cards in sequential order and writes as much as possible about the topic.

Written Language Assignments:

- Give specific instructions and outlines for writing assignments when appropriate.
- Shorten writing assignments as necessary.
- Provide story frames to help students expand their written products.
- Allow students to choose one familiar idea and generate a word bank, or give the student pictures from which to generate an idea. Once an idea is generated, have the student outline the story or topic.
- Have students bring a picture from home and write about it. They can write descriptive words or illustrate ideas; words may be combined into simple sentences.
- Incorporate graphic organizers to help generate ideas.
- Use picture cards or postcards for a "fast-forward" and "rewind" activity:
  ➤ Rewind: "Write about what happened right before this picture was taken."
  ➤ Fast-forward: "What do you think is going to happen next?"
- Let students use the writing modality that is most comfortable for them (e.g., manuscript, cursive, computer, dictation).
- Allow students to use response cards with pre-written answers.
- Do group brainstorming, learning-partner brainstorming, and then independent practice to generate ideas before writing.
- Use story maps to help students generate ideas for writing.
- When responding to questions, allow struggling students to write the answers in list form rather than writing out complete sentences or paragraphs.
- Provide students with specific examples of poor, good, and exemplary student work for their grade level.
- Avoid excessive corrections of errors in the mechanical aspects of writing. Focus on the development of ideas.
- Teach mapping skills for writing assignments.
- Before writing a story, have student answer "wh" questions *(who. what where, when, why?)* to focus their ideas.
- For writing assignments, teach the importance of beginning, middle, and end (and the use of transition words).
- Teach student to proofread; provide a checklist for this purpose.
- Tape record a student reading his or her finished story or writing assignment.

Box continues on next page

- Use key word strategies, such as the following:
  - ➤ COPS Technique
    - C   Capitalization
    - O   Overall appearance
    - P   Punctuation
    - S   Spelling
  - ➤ TOWER Strategy
    - T   Think
    - O   Order
    - W   Write
    - E   Edit
    - R   Re-write

Prewriting Stage:

- Allow a student to dictate his or her story to you or a peer.
- Have students copy material from the board or overhead.
- Allow students to illustrate their responses.
- Have students trace templates to help develop fine motor control.
- Provide tracing paper and have the student trace large objects/pictures.
- Have students practice letter formation with the use of clay, sand trays, templates, and screen spelling (described elsewhere in this book).
- Provide dot-to-dot picture activities.
- Incorporate fine motor activities such as stringing beads, pegboards, sewing cards, weaving, cutting, or clay.

Fine Motor Skills:

- Encourage the use of a tripod pencil grip.
- Encourage the use of a slant board when writing.
- Provide various sizes of wide-ruled paper.
- Place alphabet cards or strips on individual student desks.

SPELLING MODIFICATIONS

Successful spelling and writing skills are essential in the classroom. However, many students with special needs struggle with these areas. Word-processing programs and other technology tools have assisted many students, especially in the areas of spelling and assisting students who have poor handwriting. However, trouble in coming up with ideas, poor grammar skills, and slow typing speed may interfere with progress. Recent technological advances include talking word processors, which are necessary for visually impaired students and also important for students who benefit from auditory feedback to help them check for spelling errors. Here are some specific spelling modifications:

- Adjust the number of items on the vocabulary list.
- Group spelling words into word families so that spelling patterns become apparent.
- Use commonly used sight words.
- Provide for screen spelling (described elsewhere in this book). Create a 9" × 12" medium-mesh aluminum screen using materials from the hardware store. Cover the edges with masking tape or duct tape. The student places paper on top of the screen and writes the spelling words with a crayon, then traces over the letters. This tactile approach to spelling really helps struggling students.
- "Bean boggle" (described elsewhere in this book): Buy a large bag of flat, white lima beans and small zip-top bags. Print consonants on the beans a with black permanent marker, and print vowels with a red marker. Students strengthen their fine motor skills and spelling ability as they work in partners to make as many spelling words as they can using the beans.
- Use functional words common in their environment (e.g., *stop, restroom*).
- Assist students with word configuration clues (have them "box in" the letters for visual clues.
- Provide students with pictures of the vocabulary words so they have a visual representation.
- Use supplemental drill-and-practice exercises such as bingo or hangman.
- Have students practice letter formation with shaving cream, sand trays, and finger paints.
- Construct a three-dimensional word wall out of cereal boxes. Have students do a word hunt using a pointer.

MATH MODIFICATIONS

Many students struggle with math. Try some of the following modifications with your students:

- Reinforce math concepts with "real-life" situations.
- Provide students with a dictionary of math terms.
- Use drawings, diagrams, and visual demonstrations to explain concepts.
- Provide for the use of manipulatives.
- Provide for the use of a number line. You could make a large one on the floor for the students to walk on.
- Use real coins that students can count, stack, and group for solving money problems.
- Simplify vocabulary in word problems.
- Have students use egg cartons to sort various materials.
- Have students collate papers that are numbered.
- Allow students to use a calculator. Some students may benefit from a talking calculator.

Figure continues on next page

- Provide computer programs that include number recognition, matching, or sequencing.
- Play: "Hop—Step—Mat" (described elsewhere in this book): Make a grid of numbers on a shower curtain liner. Give students a math problem, and they must jump on the squares to solve it. This is a great activity for kinesthetic learners.
- Draw dotted lines between columns of problems.
- Emphasize problem-solving steps rather than the final answer.
- Number the steps in word problems. Highlight important words. Provide a visual model next to the written steps.
- Allow students to use a number stamp. This is an excellent tool for students who are having difficulty with writing a number or operation signs. Money and time stamps are also available.
- Use highlighting tape to highlight the problems to be solved, to focus attention on directions, and to help students understand place value.
- Provide a grid of paper with different colors of lines to help students line up numbers, and provide graph paper to help with place value.

STEPS FOR MODIFYING THE CURRICULUM

The simple sequence presented here describes the steps you can take to modify the content or process of instruction for specific subject matter. The step-by-step process is carefully sequenced and is adaptable depending on the age and ability levels of your students.

1. **Can the student do the same activity at the same level as peers?**

   Example: Math word problems

   IF NOT

2. **Can the student do the same activity but with adapted expectations?**

   Example: Fewer problems

   IF NOT

3. **Can the student do the same activity but with adapted expectations and materials?**

   Example: Use pictures to help the student visualize the problem

   IF NOT

4. **Can the student do a similar activity but with adapted expectations?**

   Example: Simplify the language in the word problem

   IF NOT

5. **Can the student do a similar activity but with adapted materials?**

   Example: Have the student use manipulatives to solve a problem

CHAPTER 10

Managing Inclusive Classrooms to Help All Students Learn

INTRODUCTION

How teachers present the information, engage students, select materials and tasks, interact with students, and provide multiple opportunities for flexible grouping affects the total learning environment in differentiated classrooms. This chapter will provide you with practical strategies to ensure active learning, as well as lots of ideas for grouping and cooperative group work. Flexible grouping is essential in a differentiated classroom. Keep in mind that flexible grouping can take many forms.

After assessing students' readiness, interests, learning profiles, and talents, the next step is to create a classroom environment that is interesting, encourages high-level thinking, and engages students to use key strategies to understand a concept, skill, or generalization. Flexible grouping is the key to a successful differentiated classroom. I am not suggesting that teachers forego direct instruction or whole-class work. However, productive group work is an essential tool to extend and enrich the learning of students and to meet their individual needs.

Our job as educators is to make sure that we have looked at every student as unique and special. We must teach to the individual student's strengths and maximize the potential for every student. We want children to feel connected, unique, and powerful. Placing students in flexible groups allows for changing the groups as assessments are given and the teacher sees that readiness levels have changed. In order to have groups be truly productive, we need to create the right structures and circumstances and show how productive group work is a necessary part of good teaching in inclusive classrooms.

It is important that all students are educated in a safe, secure learning environment. Predictability yields a calm environment for learning. In a safe and secure learning environment, students are not afraid to express opinions. Students become aware of their successes, which promotes self-confidence and independence. Students attribute their successes to their abilities. They take pride in individual accomplishments and also work cooperatively with others toward learning goals. Self-esteem is enhanced and students develop an optimistic view of life. Students set higher standards for themselves.

The research is clear that well-structured flexible group work is one set of strategies that teachers can use to effectively meet the needs of *all* students in a heterogeneous classroom (Cohen, 1994; Johnson & Johnson, 1999; Slavin, 1983).

If you don't use flexible grouping, it is almost impossible to differentiate instruction. That is, trying to vary instruction without grouping students according to their various entry points to learning would not be successful. A common problem is that teachers haven't been empowered with knowledge of high-quality strategies to equip them with the sophisticated range of skills and curriculum formats necessary to get the most out of flexible group work. This chapter is designed to provide you with techniques to help remedy that situation.

Unfortunately, grouping children for reading has been around for so long—with group names like the "bluebirds" and "buzzards"—that we do it without fully understanding why and how it impacts a differentiated classroom. It is important to understand the distinct difference between fixed and static "ability groups" and flexible groups. Let's take a closer look at the distinction. According to *The Literacy Dictionary: The Vocabulary of Reading and Writing* (Harris & Hodges, 1995), the distinction between these two grouping strategies is as follows:

> *ability grouping:* the placement of students according to similar levels of intelligence or achievement in some skills or subject, either within or among classes or schools; tracking; homogeneous grouping.
> *flexible grouping*: allowing students to work in differently mixed groups depending on the goal of the learning task at hand.

For teachers who are most comfortable with direct teaching via whole-class delivery of instruction, moving toward small groups and flexible grouping can be a very daunting and intimidating task. This is especially true in situations where group dynamics in the classroom are extra-lively and teachers are concerned about managing behavior and keeping learners on task.

WHY AND WHEN TO USE SMALL GROUPS

What does productive and purposeful group work look like? Odds are that not all group work you are currently having your students do should be done in a group. You need to match the right strategy with the learning task. A simple rule of thumb is that if it is a skill-building or skill-practice activity, it is best done individually or with structured learning partners rather than a group of four to six students. For example, if the learning task is to answer the questions at the end of the chapter of a textbook, or to master the three key steps of a scientific or math principle, a partner strategy would likely be more effective than small-group work.

Large-group work is more appropriate for an open-ended, thought-provoking task with multiple responses that will engage the entire group to do it thoroughly. Group tasks need to be rich and engaging, open-ended, authentic, and inclusive. Another purpose of flexible group work is to have a team goal and/or group product. It is important to make it obvious to the students that they really do need each other to solve the problem or issue or complete the task. Teachers should provide prompts and suggestions at first by noting the abilities required to do the task well.

CREATING A LEARNING ENVIRONMENT FOR SMALL GROUPS

What are some management strategies and tips for creating a learning environment that is conducive to differentiated instruction and small-group work? Remember that flexible grouping is the number one differentiation strategy to foster an engaging learning environment. It is important to establish expectations for procedures and routines before any kind of grouping can begin. The goal in designing the classroom to be conducive to small-group work is to create a structure that allows the teacher to interact quickly and easily with all students.

By changing your classroom environment, you can deliver more content in a meaningful way and have your students understand and retain more of that content. Decide on a physical setting that is conducive to small groups. What physical structure will work best for you and your students? Ask yourself the following questions as you decide on the physical arrangement of the classroom:

- Will one room arrangement work, or will multiple arrangements be necessary depending on the group activity?
- If multiple arrangements are needed, how will the class be rearranged when necessary? What will be required to accomplish rearranging the classroom?
- If multiple arrangements are needed, what routines and skills are necessary for students to learn to have the class run smoothly when we deviate from the traditional row arrangement?

If you decide that multiple arrangements will be necessary, note the following tips:

- Have students practice moving from one room arrangement to another.
- Use a signal, either a hand gesture or a sound, to notify students of the time remaining until a transition, then use the signal again when the transition needs to occur.
- Before any transition, remind students of behavioral expectations.

If your flexible grouping includes the use of learning centers, areas in the room should have clear, distinct physical boundaries if space allows. For example, there could be a work area, art area, computer center, and so forth. In addition, the workstations need to be physically accessible for all students. Desks or centers should be arranged so students can access information easily. Keep in mind that students should be physically comfortable and in a position to minimize distractions. Furthermore, learning environments should be organized so visual and auditory distractions are minimized.

Take a look around your classroom. What do you see? Faded bulletin boards that have not been changed in months? Stacks of books piled on shelves and gathering dust? Or do you see a kid-friendly environment that invites and inspires learning? Your students are guests in your classroom. How do you prepare for guests in your home? You make them feel welcome. Strive for an environment that embraces flexible grouping—that is fresh, alive, and full of vitality!

It is important to set the classroom tone for differentiation. One idea is to collect student data (learning styles, multiple intelligences, etc.) and create a Learning Profile Card for each student.

To further streamline the lesson process, think of unique ways to collect papers. For instance, the student in each group "who has the most pets" will be the "resource manager" and collect the papers from the team.

Talking to an "elbow partner" is another convenient way for students to exchange ideas. Explain to students that an "elbow partner" is the student who is next to you, behind you, or in front of you—someone within "elbow's distance."

PLANNING FOR GROUPS

Teachers need to determine how to group students based on the following:

- Ability
- Readiness, assessed through pre-lesson/activity assessment and informal "kid watching"
- Interests, which can be gathered from interest inventories, class discussions, and personal profiles
- Learning styles—how students learn best
- Multiple intelligences
- Size of group for type of activity

There are several methods teachers can use to form groups. One way is through the use of assessment data. For example, teachers might use standardized test scores, curriculum-based measurement, progress monitoring, informal assessments such as classroom observations, exit cards, action research, observation, and student self-assessment. Students could also be grouped by readiness, interest in the topic, or learning profile.

Many teachers prefer grouping students based on targeted areas of instruction. If students did poorly on a specific state standard or are struggling to understand a curriculum concept, those students might be grouped together temporarily to accelerate growth. Students might also be grouped in mixed-ability groups so that in every group there are peer tutors and supports in place for students who are struggling. Because of these factors, groups can be teacher selected, random, or student choice. In fact, if one was a fly on the wall in a classroom fully engaged in flexible grouping, one might see small groups of students of similar readiness level working together, mixed-ability groups, pairs and partners, and one-on-one interactions. There are many issues and options in planning for groups. It really depends on the purpose of the lesson and the subject matter, as well as the prior knowledge of the students.

In introducing a group activity, be very explicit in explaining instructions and giving directions. Make sure students understand what they are going to do and why they are going to do it. In other words, let them know your teaching expectations and their individual responsibilities. Model the final product for them. Establish clear time limits and provide checkpoints within those time limits. For instance, if students are going to work in small groups for 15 minutes, check in with them every 5 minutes or so to monitor understanding and to help keep them on track.

Proper planning for small group work increases the effectiveness of differentiation and supports student success. The following planning guide summarizes the considerations.

PLANNING GUIDE FOR INSTRUCTIONAL GROUPING

Identifying Purpose

What is your purpose/rationale for grouping?

Logistics

How many groups will you have? How many students in each group?
How long will students be working in their assigned groups?
How will groups rotate, and how often? Will a schedule be necessary?
How will you set up the group areas and materials in your classroom?
Will you keep routines and activities permanent, or change them throughout the
    school year?

Materials and Instruction

Will you have a teacher-led group? If so, what will be your instructional emphasis
    for this group? Will all students rotate through your group?
What materials and resources will you need for each group?

Assessment

How often will you assess students' progress in groups? Will you use the results to
    adjust groupings? If so, what will be the basis for the regroupings?
How do you plan to keep track of student work? Assessments? Record keeping?

Procedures and Management

Describe how you plan to introduce grouping to your students.
If you are working with a group, how will you ensure that you are not interrupted?
How will you facilitate smooth transitions when students rotate?
Describe how you will assign group activities (e.g., menu, contract, checklist, etc.).
How will students be asked to keep track of their work (in progress and/or
    completed)?

Other Concerns

Will students have something to do if they finish their group activity early?

METHODS OF GROUPING STUDENTS

Varying grouping strategies will better provide for the needs of individual students
and enhance student learning opportunities. I like to think in terms of providing
a daily "balanced diet" of grouping strategies depending on the content and the
desired outcomes of lessons and activities. Just as it is important to have a balanced
diet to meet our nutritional needs with daily portions of the four basic food groups,
it is also important to provide our students with a balanced diet of grouping patterns.

A good way to remember the four basic grouping patterns is with TAPS (Chapman, & King, 2003):

T = Total group
A = Alone time
P = Partner work
S = Small group

Flexible Grouping Techniques

The following list of flexible grouping techniques lists their characteristics, describes their implementation, and provides examples of each.

Random
   Overview: Students group themselves by numbers, colors, stickers, deck of cards, or other selection method.
   Implementation: This method is helpful if you want groups of equal size. It makes a good mixer activity for students to work together spontaneously.
   Example: Distribute color chips, playing cards, stickers. Students then need to find others with the same color, suit of cards, or sticker to work with.
Readiness
   Overview: Students with similar readiness levels on a specific task are grouped together.
   Implementation: Use this method when you want students to work with others at similar readiness levels, as determined by teacher observation or informal assessment to determine their entry point of learning on a specific task.
   Example: Students need content that is appropriate to their instructional level. Be flexible in placing students in these groups. For instance, a student may meet with one group that is focusing on phonics at a certain level and another group for comprehension or fluency.
Student Interest
   Overview: Students choose their groups based on their interests in a certain topic or activity.
   Implementation: Student interest is motivated by choice for learning about a topic.
   Example: In a unit about oceans, one group choice might be "Describe your favorite day at the ocean and illustrate it." Another group may have the task of listing kinds of fish in the ocean. Yet another group may choose to read a book about oceans and do a response journal, sharing with each other what they learned. After the first grouping, re-sort the groups jigsaw-style so that all students learn about facts about the ocean, types of fish in the ocean, and favorite times at the beach.
Teacher Directed
   Overview: The teacher balances groups heterogeneously to include leaders, followers, recorders, and reporters based on student social skills.
   Implementation: Each student has a different role to perform within the group in order to complete a group task.
   Example: In preparing to share information about the topic with the larger group, one student might read, another one takes notes, another records the discussion in pictures, and one is the reporter for the group.

Please see Figures for examples of elementary and secondary role group cards.

Task
> *Overview:* Students successful in completing certain kinds of tasks are grouped together.
>
> *Implementation:* Enables students to use their strongest modality/learning style.
>
> *Example:* Students who are visual learners are grouped together to create a storyboard of the story that was read. Others might work on a Venn diagram to compare and contrast the main characters of the story.

Knowledge of Subject
> *Overview:* Students with specific knowledge of a given subject or topic are grouped together.
>
> *Implementation:* Students share information and gain new insights and background knowledge about a topic to become more proficient in that area.
>
> *Example:* In studying ancient Egypt, some students could focus on their knowledge of pyramids, some on food and family life, and some on rulers and leaders of the time.

Skill Building
> *Overview:* Students who are lacking a specific skill or who need more work in a specific area are grouped together.
>
> *Implementation:* Teachers design group interventions to teach a certain skill to those who need more practice.
>
> *Example:* A group in math class could focus on operation signs or order of operations in solving math problems; a group in English class could focus on phonics review; a group in science class could focus on steps in the scientific method.

Student Choice
> *Overview:* Students are provided an opportunity to group themselves.
>
> *Implementation:* Students are allowed to choose their own groups, especially when success is not dependent upon choice. This works best when used as an enrichment activity to build upon the total-group, teacher-directed lesson.
>
> *Example:* As an extension to a unit on the Civil War, display several different titles of books about the war. Let the students choose their books, then they form literature response groups to discuss their selections.

MANAGEMENT PROCEDURES FOR GROUP WORK

Ideas to Consider

The keys to successful flexible grouping in your classroom are carefully designed procedures and routines. Many teachers give up on grouping because "chaos reigns supreme" when the students get out of their seats. Explain all procedures one step at a time and be sure that you model clear expectations for students so that they clearly know what they need to do and how to do it.

Have a strong idea of why a differentiated classroom is important, and convey this to your students and their parents. In addition, keep the following tips in mind:

- *Always* monitor groups by floating and asking questions. Help students troubleshoot. Refrain from giving solutions.
- Use a clipboard as you move through the room to monitor student performance.
- As students are working in groups, write comments/suggestions to them on sticky notes to provide them with quick feedback without interrupting the group process.
- Appoint jobs in the groups for each group member, such as leader, recorder, time keeper, and organizer.
- With students, develop expectations for working in groups. Create a rubric of criteria and have all members of each group assess themselves at the end of each group-work session. After they have finished, go around the room and agree or disagree with groups' self-assessment. (Possible expectations include the following: On Task, Sharing Ideas, Cooperating, Using Time Wisely.)
- Keep in mind the attention span of your students, and design group or independent work accordingly—pacing is critical.
- Use specific "anchor activities" to engage your learners so they experience success and you can focus on meeting individual needs.
- Make sure your directions are clear, succinct, and presented in multiple ways, if necessary.
- Create management signals and processes for your students to work independently while they are waiting for help from you.
- Scaffold increasing responsibility for your students.
- Constantly evaluate your procedures and routines for greater clarity.

Expectations for Your Students

You need to expect that the students will follow the *procedures and routines.* in addition to modeling these, have the students rehearse them. You could even use a stopwatch and say: "It took us 30 seconds yesterday to get into our groups. Let's break that record today." This motivates the students. Share management responsibilities with the students by appointing classroom managers or resident experts to distribute and collect materials and to monitor group work.

Another technique that can facilitate management is "see three before me," discussed in an earlier chapter. With this technique, students are not allowed to come and ask you for help until they have first checked with three other students. For this purpose, consider having three or four students serves as "classroom experts" who are to be consulted before asking the teacher for help. Keep a list of these classroom experts posted and rotate them regularly so all students get chances to be the expert.

It is also helpful to *rehearse directions* for new learning formats first with the whole class, and to set expectations, before asking students to carry them out in differentiated groups. *Location* of the varied workspaces also needs to be made clear.

What do students do while they are *waiting for help*? Have some "emergency task" cards ready that they can use until help arrives. Similarly, strategies need to be planned for when the group finishes the assignment. Chances are, all groups will not finish at the same time. One suggestion is to present a menu of tasks for "early finishers." Students who have finished then choose one and work quietly until group time is over.

It is also helpful to establish signals and procedures that are used for progress monitoring without students having to leave their seats or groups. I have found it helpful to create a three-sided table tent labeled: Hard at Work, HELP!, and Finished. For students who display "Finished," check to see if it is quality work before they move on to anchor or other choice activities. Another variation on this idea is for students to use red, yellow, and green plastic cups to indicate that they are working just fine (green), stuck and in need of help (red), or finished (yellow).

For a smooth-running class, leave nothing to the imagination. Be sure to set aside a place or a procedure for *completed work*. In addition, it is always helpful for students to evaluate how they worked as a group. It could be something as simple as a chart noting "what worked well," "what did not work well," and "why." This process helps students become more accountable for their time together.

Discussing appropriate *noise level* expectations for various tasks can be very helpful as well. What noise levels are appropriate with partner talk, table talk, presentation talk, and independent work? You can assist students in maintaining the expected noise level by using a scale of 1–5, with 1 being a whisper and 5 being group discussion.

Furthermore, *schedules* are an important expectation to facilitate group work. Schedules supply visual support for routines for both you and your students. Clearly post a schedule so that everyone knows where to be and what to do. A schedule also helps everyone understand the duration of activities. Individual schedules may be used for students who have additional routines or who may need a more individualized way to access daily routine information.

Strategies for Effective Group Processes

Establish ground rules. In order for students to behave appropriately and stay on task during small-group work, they have to be taught how to work in a group. Students have been trained over the years to sit at desks lined up in rows and passively receive information. Many, if not most, students have no idea how to work in a group. If they do have experience with group work, it might be quite limited because schools still teach primarily through a direct teaching, whole-class model. So when students are suddenly asked to work in a group, they often misbehave and mismanage their time. They simply don't know how to do small-group work.

Consequently, teachers need to teach students how to work in a group. The first step in the process is to establish ground rules and norms for interaction. These are the guidelines that must be enforced by teachers and students themselves in order for group work to be effective. Ground rules should encourage positive collaborative behaviors among all students. In my experience, students abide by rules best when they have a part in making them. Guidelines/ground rules need to be posted in the classroom so students can readily refer to them. If students or teachers believe that additional rules are needed, they can be added later.

A very effective technique for teaching students appropriate small-group behavior is to have students take an active role in identifying what appropriate behavior actually looks like. It's worth taking the time to do some role-playing with the students to show the difference between an ineffective group and an effective group. Another very effective strategy is to have students give their input on inappropriate behavior, for example, putting other students down or laughing at a group member's ideas. Students are more likely to comply if they have agreed on reasonable behavior and consequences.

Some suggested ground rules are the following:

- We will start and stop on time.
- Practice respect for yourself and others.
- Come prepared to do your part.
- Be a good listener.
- Provide positive comments rather than putdowns.
- Make sure that everyone gets a chance to speak.
- Critique ideas rather than people.
- Stay on task.
- Let people finish talking without interruptions.
- Help others when you can.
- Do your personal best.

Procedures for Group Routines

When you are using various grouping techniques to enhance differentiation and to be more inclusive of your struggling students, it is also important to vary the kinds of lessons presented. That involves paying attention to different modes of teacher output and student input. Timing of the group work is also critical to a successful differentiated classroom. Perhaps you will need to shorten some assignments, focusing on content and mastery of concepts, not quantity. For longer assignments, it is helpful to allow breaks in work time.

For greater clarity, avoid giving multiple directions at one time. Show examples of completed assignments to affirm your expectations. Review students' prior knowledge at the beginning of the lesson (see the section on assessment in this chapter). In order to engage all learners, you need to set realistic expectations based on their different entry points to learning.

Begin all lessons with an overview and end with a summary and student reflection. Give the students time to "chunk and chew" the information. Deliver whole-class instruction in small chunks (10–12 minutes) and allow 2 minutes of "chew time" for them to process the information they just learned. They could share a key idea with the "elbow partners" next to them, or they could meet with a "clock buddy" partner (discussed elsewhere in this book). Perhaps you would like them to do a "quick write" of the main ideas or draw a picture or symbol of what they found memorable.

Balancing Small-Group Instruction

Every day, each student is involved in some whole-class instruction and direct teaching. It is important during these times to be very explicit in the content or strategies that you are sharing and to model them for the students.

The focus on this chapter is small-group instruction. There is not an exact recipe for how many times small groups should be used to extend and enrich the whole-class lesson and to provide extra practice time regarding the concepts. However, at least every week, all students at every grade level should be engaged in small, flexible groups. I strive to do it on a daily basis once the routines and procedures are established. The bottom line is to meet the needs of *all* of your students—including struggling and advanced learners.

You will have to plan to fit small-group instruction into your schedule, just like you need to plan things in your personal life that you would like to accomplish. Because you need to consider the students and the curriculum, allow for some flexibility in your schedule. It would be difficult to meet with every group during every group-work session, unless you have an instructional assistant in your classroom The purpose of effective small-group instruction in your classroom is to better meet the individual needs of your students in an active and engaging way to accelerate their learning.

Your teaching role changes during small-group time. You facilitate, rather than dictate, the outcomes. You assist and support where needed and foster greater self-management among the students. This is a time for them to problem solve, collaborate, and apply the strategies that you have taught them.

All curricular content areas are conducive to small-group work. At the beginning, I would start with just one subject at a time. When you feel that the process has been mastered, then you can successfully utilize small groups in other subject areas. Note the following features of effective versus ineffective small-group instruction.

Effective Small-Group Instruction

- Uses assessment data to create lesson plans and determine the groups
- Keeps groups small, preferably three to four students per group; uses pairs when appropriate
- Uses flexible groups that can change in configuration as students grow, test out of a curriculum section, choose activities based on the type of activity required, and so forth
- Gears instructional materials toward student readiness levels when activities are not based on differentiating by process or student profile

Ineffective Small-Group Instruction

- Has students in groups, but the teacher directs all activity
- Keeps students in the same groups continually, usually ability groups (This is actually "tracking" within a class.)
- Uses the same materials with all students in all groups
- Uses the same independent work assignments for the entire class
- Uses small groups to complete worksheets, and more worksheets, and more worksheets

What Does Self-Management Look Like?

All kids need to be accountable for learning what the group is together to work on; this aspect often is left out of group work. A simple rule of thumb for students is as follows: "Your teammates can help you learn, but you need to ultimately go to bat for yourself." For example, if the group is together to design an advertising campaign for a political candidate (a team product), each individual student must write a one-page summary of the thinking behind the campaign as a homework assignment. The following are powerful strategies to encourage individual accountability:

- Assign individual homework based on the "big idea" of the group work task.
- Randomly select one or two students to be the spokesperson(s) for the group.
- Have students complete individual quizzes or tests over the group-work material.

- Have students use the "ambassadors strategy" to share information between groups.
- Use structured roles for each student within groups, and monitor to ensure that students perform them.

What Are Your Expectations for Student Self-Management?

Consider the following aspects of self-managed students and how much more smoothly your classroom would run with learners displaying these characteristics.

Self-Managed Students Know

- How to keep materials organized
- What the behavior expectations are
- What to do if:
  - ➢ They need help
  - ➢ They need to leave the room
  - ➢ The teacher is with someone else
  - ➢ They are working with partners
- What to do when assigned task is finished
  - ➢ Where their finished work goes
  - ➢ What they will work on until everyone has finished
- How to problem solve
  - ➢ Where to find information
  - ➢ What to do if they need materials
  - ➢ How to handle conflict with another student

You can assist students with self-management by making sure that all materials are in an appropriate place for distribution. It is also helpful to have role cards preprinted for distribution. A rubric of expectations should be created and shared (more information on this is presented in the assessment section of this chapter). For teacher-assigned groups, create a student group list. You need to decide how many will be in each group and how you want them to accomplish the task. Goals of the small-group assignment should be written out and agreed upon. Providing a checklist of procedures for students is also helpful.

IDEAS FOR ACTIVE LEARNING

LEARNING-GO-ROUND

Overview

Learning-Go-Round is a structure designed for small groups of students to activate their learning about a particular topic. It works best with a topic that can be divided into a series of subtopics or a series of questions about a topic. Large sheets of chart paper are posted around the room. Each sheet has a different subtopic or question. This active, kinesthetic strategy gets your students up and moving as they share their responses about a particular topic. This strategy will energize and engage your students.

In small groups, students rotate from one chart to the next to brainstorm what they know about each question or subtopic. Each group has a different-colored marker to contribute ideas. Groups "cruise" around to all the charts and return to their original charts to see what other groups have added (Kagan. 1994).

Implementation

Use the following steps to implement this strategy:

- Write a question or subtopic on each chart.
- Divide students into small groups.
- Give each group a different-colored marker and send them to a chart to start.
- Choose a recorder and a reporter for each group.
- Direct the students to brainstorm responses to the question or subtopics.
- Give them a specific time period (3–5 minutes).
- Students stop when you give them a signal.
- Tell recorders to the give markers to another student in the group, and each group rotates one chart to the right.
- Repeat the previous steps.
- Continue until each group has brainstormed responses to all the topics or questions.
- Each group "cruises" back to the original chart and reviews what others have contributed.
- Students can then group the responses into categories or select the three most significant ideas.
- Groups report to the whole class.

Variations

- Each subtopic or question can be put on a clipboard. Have the students pass the clipboard from group to group.
- Students can remain at their tables in small groups; the charts can then "cruise" around the room from group to group.
- For primary grades, charts can be on the floor and students can draw pictures for their responses.
- As a summarizer, students can review and reinforce material already studied by listing what they know or by writing questions for the upcoming test.

Adapted from Kagan, 1994

WALK AND TALK TOUR

Overview

The Walk and Talk Tour is a small-group strategy that is particularly effective when introducing content that contains provocative ideas, important quotes, complex passages, or confusing information. These passages, quotes, and/or ideas are written on individual charts, and students take a walking, talking "tour" from chart to chart as

Box continues on next page

they discuss, interpret, and extend the ideas presented. The purposes of this activity is to create a "need to know," set a goal for the learning, raise curiosity, and boost comprehension when the students encounter the same passages or quotes in the text or story they are about to read.

The teacher chooses the passage or quote for posting on the charts. Charts are then mounted around the room and numbered. Small groups of students are formed and are assigned to each chart. Groups spend 3 to 5 minutes at each chart, where they discuss, interpret, and react to the quote or idea presented. Their reactions can be verbal or in writing. Students then move on to the next chart and repeat the process with a new quote or passage. This process is continued until they have had a chance to visit all of the charts. When they return to their seats, they discuss and summarize their reactions to each passage.

Implementation

Use the following steps to implement this strategy:

- Write a passage, quotation, statement, or an idea on each chart.
- Divide students into small groups.
- Assign each group to a different chart to start their walking, talking tour.
- Direct the students to brainstorm responses to the quotes or passages.
- Give them a specific time period (3–5 minutes).
- Provide them with prompts to discuss verbally or in writing.
- Students stop when you give them a signal.
- Each group rotates one chart to the right.
- Repeat the previous steps.
- Continue until each group has brainstormed responses to all the quotations or passages.
- Groups report to the whole class.

Possible Prompts to Use

The following are suggestions for prompts:

- "This reminds me of . . ."
- "I am beginning to wonder . . ."
- "I now realize . . ."
- "This means . . ."
- "Some problems this might cause are . . ."
- "I don't agree with . . ."
- "I am confused by . . ."
- "Advantages/disadvantages of this are . . ."
- "This sounds like . . ."
- "This looks like . . ."
- "One way to interpret this is . . ."
- "A question this raises is . . ."
- "Causes/effects might be . . ."
- "Some problems this might cause are . . ."
- "Some consequences of this might be . . ."

Variations

Before the students take the walking and talking tour, model and suggest ways to react to the charts, quotes, and/or passages (Adapted from Kagan, 1994).

Jigsaw tour— If time is limited, form teams that are made up of the same numbers of students as there are charts posted around the room. One student representative from each group goes to the corresponding chart and discusses it and then returns to the home group to share what the learning.

CLOCK BUDDIES

Overview

Clock buddies is a structure designed to be an efficient and effective process for pairs of students working together. This structure can provide a necessary "brain break" in your lesson as students interact with each other and share their ideas. Clock buddies is a great way to pair off students for any activity or discussion. The good news about clock buddies is that once students have completed their clock buddies sheets, they can be used all semester long.

Implementation

The teacher makes copies of the clock buddies sheet shown in Figure 10.1 and distributes it to students.

Figure 10.1. Clock Buddies Sheet

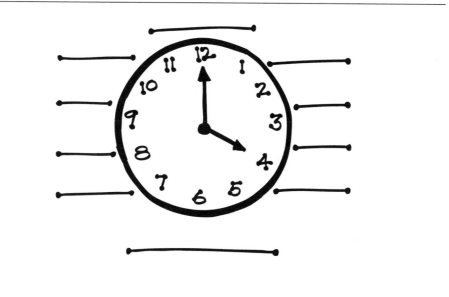

Box continues on next page

Have students take their clock buddies sheets with them as they travel around the room finding other students and making appointments for each time on the clock sheet. Be sure to explain that each time a student makes an appointment at a given time, he or she must enter his or her name on the other student's sheet at that same time—the clock times must agree. For instance, if Mike is Ann's 9 o'clock appointment, then Ann needs to have Mike's name at her 9 o'clock time slot. Give the students a finite amount of time to fill in their sheets. Play lively music in the background to keep the pace up.

You now have an instant way to pair up your students. This comes in very handy when a state change or a "brain break" is needed to process the information learned. For instance, after a lesson in science, you could say, "Find your 2 o'clock partner and share with them the three main ideas from this chapter."

Please note that the time on the clock buddies sheet does not have to correspond to the time on the classroom clock. This means that you do not have to extend the school day until midnight or start at 7 o'clock in the morning!

For younger students, you might want to have them fill in one time slot at a time for greater understanding. An example of this variation would be to say, "Students, please find a 1 o'clock partner." After all students have completed this time slot on the sheet, you proceed to the other time slots around the clock.

Variations

Students could use other structures, such as seasonal partners (e.g., winter, summer, spring, fall), day and night partners, and so on.

GROUPING "ROUNDUP" OF IDEAS

Overview

There are multiple ways to use random grouping strategies in your classroom to promote differentiation and engagement. The key to the success of these grouping strategies is careful planning of procedures and routines. Always define the parameters of the structure, providing the students with clear outcomes and a specific time limit. Once they are in their groups, give specific directions.

Implementation

There are many different ways to use random grouping in your classroom. Some of these follow.

Color-Coded Buddies

Students are asked to stand and mix and mingle to the music. Each student is to find a partner who is wearing a similar color to the one he or she is wearing. Once they find their color-coded partners, they wait for further directions to respond to the lesson.

Address Buddies

Ask students to think of their home address. Then ask them to concentrate on the first digit of the address (numbers from 1 to 9). They should stand and flash that number with their fingers until they find a group of three to four others with the same first digit. If they have difficulty finding someone who shares the same digit, they can go to the "next-door neighbor" for a visit (one digit higher or one digit lower). After address buddies are formed, the teacher gives directions for the discussion or activity.

The Eyes Have It!

This random grouping strategy involves the students mixing and mingling to music around the room. They need to find someone who has the same color of eyes as they do. That student will be their partner.

Deal Me In!

In this grouping strategy, the teacher needs to count how many students are in class that day and then count out the corresponding number of cards. For instance, if 28 students are present, the teacher pulls out seven sets of four cards from the deck and shuffles them. The cards should be dealt to the students facedown. Students find the others who share their number card or face card (e.g., all the 6s work together, all the kings work together, etc.) The teacher then assigns roles based on the suits of the cards—for example, the heart is the facilitator, the diamond is the reporter, the ace is the recorder, and the club is the observer. In this way, not only are the groups randomly formed, but their respective roles in the group are randomly assigned as well. This technique is very fast and efficient.

Comic Strip Groups

This is a fun, interactive way to do random grouping with your students. For small groups, use the daily comics in your newspaper, which are usually three to four frames each. For larger groups, use the Sunday comics, which are usually six to eight frames each. Select the comic strips and then cut them out into individual frames. Count out how many students are in class that day and select that many comic frames, then mix them up. Distribute the comic frames to the students. At the signal, students mix and mingle to music and find the other students who share a frame from the comic strip. For instance, all of the "Doonesbury" strips will be a team, and all of the "Peanuts" comic strips will be another team. Once the students find their matches, ask them to arrange the frames in the correct sequence to tell the story. After that is complete, give them directions for the activity or lesson. Comic strip frames can be laminated and mounted on construction paper to use multiple times.

Valentine Pairs

Collect and recycle valentines. Have the students find their "Valentine matches" to form pairs. A helpful hint is to wait until the day after Valentine's Day and buy the Valentines at a deep discount!

Salt and Pepper Pairs

Prepare a list of word pairs that are commonly used together and duplicate the list or write the words on cards. Cut them apart and mix them up. Cards are then dealt out to the students. At the signal, they are to mingle around the room and find a "match" These learning partners will now form a pair for the pair-share discussion that follows. Some examples of matches include the following:

salt	pepper	shoes	socks
spaghetti	meatballs	rain	umbrella
knife	fork	wash	dry
coffee	tea	stop	go
bacon	eggs	comb	brush
pencil	paper	aunt	uncle
sweet	sour	you	me
bees	honey	heart	soul
close	open	peanut butter	jelly
moon	sun	table	chairs
cold	hot	sugar	cream

ASSESSMENT OF GROUPS

We know that authentic assessment is much more than just weekly tests to put a score in the grade book. The typical view of teach, teach, test has now changed. The students and the curriculum need to be at the core of assessment. Students can demonstrate their strengths and knowledge in a variety of ways. Ongoing and informative assessment needs to be the focus of a differentiated program.

It is a process of assessing students before, during, and after the lesson or unit. In the before phase, you determine their background knowledge and their entry points to learning about the topic. This phase is the pre-assessment. Formative assessment occurs during the learning process as you track each student's progress. The purpose of the assessment is to see if students have met the lesson's goals, or achieved lesson mastery. Therefore, a summative assessment is also necessary.

There are many **options for implementing ongoing assessment within a classroom as a means** to use student- and teacher-generated data sources as a guide for grouping students. The following lists note examples of each.

Student-Generated Data Sources

- Journal entries
- Short-answer test responses
- Open-response test results
- Homework completion
- Notebook checks
- Class participation
- Previously completed projects
- Problem-solving skills

Teacher-Generated Data Sources

- Anecdotal records
- Teacher observation
- Class discussion
- Rubrics
- Exit cards
- Individualized assessment
- Student–teacher conferencing
- Observation of small-group interaction
- Data collected during class discussions

On-the-Spot Assessment Techniques

- The 0, 3, 5 finger response, or "give me five" assessment, shown in Figure 10.2

Figure 10.2. "Give Me Five" Assessment

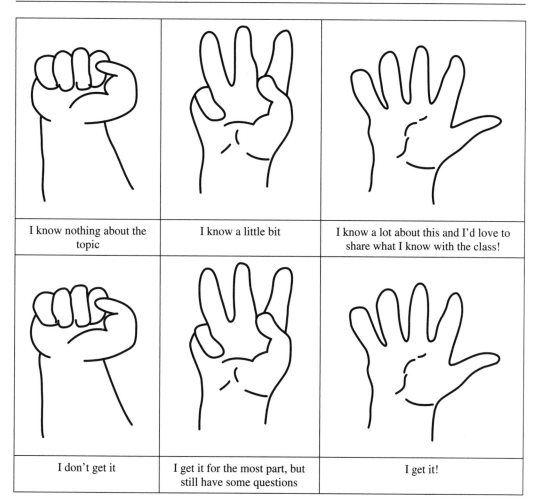

I know nothing about the topic	I know a little bit	I know a lot about this and I'd love to share what I know with the class!
I don't get it	I get it for the most part, but still have some questions	I get it!

- Use of individual white boards
  - ➤ Provide a dry-erase marker or wipe-off crayon as well as a sock or fabric scrap for wiping the board and storing the marker or crayon.
  - ➤ The teacher asks the class a question, and students write their responses on their white boards.
  - ➤ After allowing time for students to write their responses, the teacher asks the students to hold up their boards. At a glance, the teacher can check for understanding and see how *all* students are doing.
  - ➤ This also stops students from blurting out the answer, and allows those who need processing time to finally get that time!

Exit Cards

Exit cards (a.k.a. "tickets to leave") are used to gather information on student readiness levels, understanding of concepts just taught, interests, and/or learning profiles.

The teacher hands students index cards or a short three-question set at the end of the lesson or class. With index cards, the teacher might ask students to answer or respond to a question or prompt geared toward providing the teacher with the relevant information, whether it's understanding or student interests. The teacher might also use a ready-made set of questions preprinted on paper. Each student must complete the index card or the three-question set and turn it in before leaving the classroom or before a transition to another class activity.

The teacher then reviews student responses and uses the cards to determine instructional groups based on criteria that would best support the goals of the small-group activity.

Test-Taking Tips

There are some techniques that can help put your struggling readers more at ease with the assessment process. Allow test taking using audio or video formats for your auditory learners. Using a short-answer format works better than long essay responses. Other students can succeed with some technical support, such as a calculator or spellchecker. These students still need to demonstrate computation and processing skills as well as spelling skills; however, this technical assistance helps them find the answers more swiftly.

For struggling students, it is important to directly teach test-taking techniques. During the testing situation, create a quiet environment with few distractions. Vary the test formats in the differentiated classroom—for instance, oral tests, take-home tests, and multiple-choice tests. Just as there are multiple ways of knowing, there are also multiple ways of showing. Make sure to preteach the vocabulary used on the test or provide a word bank for students use. Because many struggling readers also have challenges with writing, allow students to check or circle the correct answer instead of writing it out.

In the assessment processes of a differentiated classroom, it is important to allow for various products as long as they meet the established criteria. For example, one student may choose to do a story map or poster instead of a traditional book report.

References

Allington, R. L. (1994). The schools we have. The schools we need. *Reading Teacher, 48*(1), 14–29.

Allington, R. L. (2002). *Schools that work: Where all children read and write.* Boston: Allyn & Bacon.

Allington, R. L., & Walmsley, S. A. (Eds.). (1995). *No quick fix: Rethinking literacy programs in American schools.* New York: Teachers College Press.

Alvermann, D. E., & Boothby, P. R. (1986). Children's transfer of graphic organizer instruction. *Reading Psychology, 7*(2), 87–100.

Anderson, N. J. (2002). *What research has to say about reading instruction.* Newark, DE: International Reading Association.

Bandura, A. (1977). Self-efficacy: Toward a unifying theory of behavioral change. *Psychological Review, 84,* 191–215.

Bandura, A. (1994). Self-efficacy. In V. S. Ramachaudran (Ed.), *Encyclopedia of human behavior, 4.* New York: Academic Press, pp. 71–81.

Baumeister, R. F., Campbell, J. D., Krueger, J. I., & Vohs, K. D. (2005). Exploding the self-esteem myth. *Scientific American, 292,* 84–92.

Beninghof, A. (1998). *Senseable strategies: Including diverse learners through multisensory strategies.* Frederick, CO: Sopris West.

Birch, B. M. (2002). *English L2 reading: Getting to the bottom.* Mahwah, NJ: Erlbaum.

Brozo, W. G., & Simpson, L. (2007). *Content literacy: Honoring diversity & building competence.* Upper Saddle River, NJ: Merrill/Prentice-Hall.

Bruer, J. T. (1991). The brain and childhood development: Time for some critical thinking. *Public Health Reports, 113*(5), 98–387.

Bulgren, J., Schumaker, J. B., & Deshler, D. D. (1988). Effectiveness of concept teaching routine in enhancing the performance of LD students in secondary-level mainstream classes. *Learning Disability Quarterly, 11*(1), 3–17.

Chapman, C., & King, R. (2003). *Differentiated Instructional Strategies for Reading in the Content Areas.* Thousand Oaks, CA: Corwin Press.

Coffield, F., Moseley, D., Hall, E., & Ecclestone, K. (2004). Learning styles and pedagogy in post-16 learning: A systematic and critical review. Learning and Skills Research Centre. Available at www.lsda.org.uk/files/PDF/1543.pdf

Cohen, Elizabeth G. (1994) Designing Groupwork: Strategies for the Heterogeneous Classroom, second edition. New York: Teachers College Press.

Coleman, J., Bradley, L., & Donovan, C. (2012). Visual representations in second graders' information book compositions. *The Reading Teacher, 66*(1), 31–35.

Comfort, R. (1990). On the idea of curriculum modification by teachers. *Academic Therapy, 25*(4), 397–405.

Cooper, D. (1997). *Literacy: Helping children construct meaning* (3rd ed.). Boston: Houghton Mifflin.

Cowan, Gregory, and Elizabeth Cowan Neeld. *Writing.* New York: Wiley, 1980.

Davey, B. (1983). Think-aloud: Modeling the cognitive processes of reading comprehension. *Journal of Reading, 27*(1), 44–47.

Dennison, P. E., & Dennison, G. (1998). *Brain gym: Teacher's edition.* Ventura, CA: Edu-Kinesthetics.

Duffy-Hester, A. (2002). *Preparing reading professionals. Teaching struggling readers in elementary school classrooms: A review of classroom reading programs and principles of instruction.* Newark, DE: International Reading Association.

Dunn, R. (1990). Understanding the Dunn and Dunn learning styles model and the need for individual diagnosis and prescription. *Journal of Reading, Writing, and Learning Disabilities International, 6,* 223–247.

Dweck, C. S. (2000). *Self-theories: Their role in motivation, personality and development.* Philadelphia, PA: Psychology Press.

Dweck, C. S. (2006). *Mindset: The new psychology of success.* New York: Random House.

Felder, R. M., & Silverman, L. K. (1988). Learning and teaching styles in engineering education. *Engineering Education, 78*(7), 674–681.

Fisher, D., & Ivey, G. (2006). When thinking skills trump reading skills. *Educational Leadership, 64,* 16–21.

Foorman, B. R., Francis, D. J., Fletcher, J. M., Schatschneider, C., & Mehta, P. (1998). The role of instruction in learning to read: Preventing reading failure in at-risk children. *Journal of Educational Psychology, 90,* 37–55.

Foorman, B. R., & Torgesen, J. (2001). Critical elements of classroom and small group instruction promote reading success in all children. *Learning Disabilities Research and Practice, 16*(4), 203–212.

Geva, E., & Siegel, L. S. (2000). Orthographic and cognitive factors in the concurrent development of basic reading skills in two languages. *Reading and Writing: An Interdisciplinary Journal, 12,* 1–30.

Gickling, E., & Rosenfield, S. (1995). Best practices in curriculum-based assessment. In A. Thomas & J. Grimes (Eds.), *Best practices in school psychology* (3rd ed., pp. 587–595). Bethesda, MD: National Association of School Psychologists.

Gregory, G., & Chapman, C. (2002). *Differentiated instructional strategies: One size doesn't fit all.* Thousand Oaks, CA: Corwin Press.

Gunning, T. G. (2001). *Building words: A resource manual for teaching word analysis and spelling strategies.* Boston: Allyn & Bacon.

Hannaford, C. (1995). *Smart moves: Why learning is not all in the head.* Marshall, NC: Great Ocean.

Harris, T., & Hodges, R. (1995). *The Literacy Dictionary: The vocabulary of reading and writing.* Newark, DE: International Reading Association.

Harste, J., Short, K., & Burke, C. (1988). *Creating classrooms for authors.* Portsmouth, NH: Heinemann.

Harvey, S., & Goudvis, A. (2007). *Strategies that work: Teaching comprehension for understanding and engagement.* Portland, ME: Stenhouse Publishers.

Hawk, T. F., & Shah, A. J. (2007). Using learning style instruments to enhance student learning. *Decision Sciences Journal of Innovative Education, 5*(1), 1–20.

Hoyt, L. (1999). *Revisit, reflect, retell.* Portsmouth, NH: Heinemann.

Idol, L., & Croll, V. J. (1987). Story-mapping training as a means of improving reading comprehension. *Learning Disabilities Quarterly, 10*(3), 214–229.

Jensen, E. (1998). *Teaching with the brain in mind.* Alexandria, VA: Association for Supervision and Curriculum Development.

Jensen, E. (2000). *Learning with the brain in mind.* San Diego: The Brain Store.

Johnson, D. W., Johnson, R. T., Holubec, Ed., & Roy, P. (1984). *Circles of learning.* Alexandria, VA: Association for Supervision and Curriculum Development.

Johnson, D. W., & Johnson, R. T. (1999). *Learning together and alone: Cooperative, competitive, and individualistic learning.* Boston: Allyn & Bacon.

Juel, C. (1988). Learning to read and write: A longitudinal study of fifty-four children from first through fourth grades. *Journal of Educational Psychology, 80*(4), 437–447.

Kagan, S. (1994). *Cooperative Learning, Resources for Teachers.* San Juan Capistrano, CA: Kagan Cooperative Learning.

Kagan, S., & Kagan, M. (2004). *The Structural Approach: Six Keys to Cooperative Learning.* S. Sharan, Handbook of Cooperative Learning Methods. Westport, CT: Greenwood Press.

Kagan, S., Kagan, M. & Kagan, L. (2000). Reaching English/Language Arts Standards through Cooperative Learning: Providing for ALL Learners in General Education Classrooms. Port Chester, NY: National Professional Resources, Inc.

Kinoshita, H. (1997). Run for your brain's life. *Brain Work, 7*(1), 8.

Klingner, J. J., & Vaughn, S. (1996). Reciprocal teaching of reading comprehension strategies for students with learning disabilities who use English as a Second Language. *The Elementary Journal, 96*(3), 275–293.

Kolodner, J. (2004). Facilitating the learning of design practices: Lessons learned from an inquiry into science education. *Journal of Industrial Teacher Education, 39*(3), 1–31.

Kostelnik, M. J., Soderman, A. K., & Whiten, A. P. (2004). Developmentally appropriate curriculum: Best practices in early childhood education (3rd ed.). Columbus, OH: Pearson, Merrill/Prentice Hall.

Kuczala M., & Lengel, T. (2010). *The kinesthetic classroom: Teaching and learning through movement.* Thousand Oaks, CA: Corwin.

Kuhn, M. R., & Stahl, S. A. (2003). Fluency: A review of developmental and remedial practices. *Journal of Educational Psychology, 95,* 3–21.

Learning First Alliance. (1998). *Every child reading: An action plan.* Washington, DC: Author.

Lee, J., Grigg, W., and Donahue, P. (2007). *The Nation's Report Card: Reading 2007* (NCES 2007-496). National Center for Education Statistics, Institute of Education Sciences, U.S. Department of Education, Washington, D.C.

Lipson, M. Y., & Wixson, K. K. (2003). *Assessment and instruction of reading and writing disability: An interactive approach* (3rd ed.). Boston: Allyn & Bacon.

Lovett, M. W., Lacerenza, L., Borden, S. L., Frijters, J. C., Steinbach, K. A., & De Palma, M. (2000). Components of effective remediation for developmental reading disability: Combining phonological and strategy-based instruction to improve outcomes. *Journal of Educational Psychology, 92,* 263–283.

Lyon, G. R. (1998). Why reading is not a natural process. *Educational Leadership, 54,* 14–18.

Lyon, G. Reid. "Why Reading Is Not a Natural Process." *LDA Newsbriefs,* January/February 2000.

Masera, R. M. (2010, January 1). Effects of Traditional versus Tactual/Kinesthetic versus Interactive-Whiteboard Instruction on Primary Students' Vocabulary Achievement- and Attitude-Test Scores. *ProQuest LLC,* Available at EBSCO*host.*

McLaughlin, M., & Overturf, B. J. (2013). *The Common ore: Teaching students on grades 6–12 to meet the reading standards.* Newark, DE: International Reading Association.

McTighe, J., & Wiggins, G. (2005). *Understanding By Design.* Alexandria, VA: Association for Supervision and Curriculum Development.

Merkley, D. M., & Jeffries, D. (2001). Guidelines for implementing a graphic organizer. *The Reading Teacher, 54*(4), 350–357.

Miller, M. (2005). Teaching and Learning in Affective Domain. In M. Orey (Ed.), Emerging perspectives on learning, teaching, and technology. Available at www. projects.coe.uga.edu/epltt/

Morgan, C., & Tam, M. (1999). Unraveling the complexities of distance education student attrition. *Distance Education, 20*(1), 96–108.

Moss, B. (2004). Teaching expository text structures through information trade book retellings. *Reading Teacher, 57*(8), 710–718.

National Reading Panel. (Panel). Report of the National Reading Panel: Teaching children to read. Report of the subgroups. Washington, DC: U.S. Department of Health and Human Services, National Institute of Health.

Nave, B. (1990). Self-esteem: The key to student success. National Dropout Prevention Center. Available at www.ndpc-n.org/publica/solu_strat/5503.pdf

Nist, S.L., & Kirby, K. (1986). Teaching comprehension and study strategies through modeling and thinking aloud. Reading Research and Instruction, 25, 254–264.

Ozga, L., & L. Sukhnandan, L. (1998). Undergraduate non-completion: Developing an explanatory model. *Higher Educational Quarterly, 52*(3), 316–333.

Palincsar, A. S., & Brown, A. L. (1986). Interactive teaching to promote independent learning from text. *The Reading Teacher, 39,* 771–777.

Paris, S. G., Wasik, B. A., & Turner, J. C. (1991). The development of strategic readers. In R. Barr, M. L. Kamil, P. Mosenthal, & P. D. Pearson (Eds.), *Handbook of reading research* (Vol. II, pp. 609–640). Mahwah, NJ: Lawrence Erlbaum.

Pearson, P. D. (1981). Asking questions about stories. In *Ginn Occasional Papers: Writings in reading and language arts* (Monograph No. 15). Lexington, MA: Ginn & Co. Reprinted in A. J. Harris & E. R. Sipay (Eds.), *Readings in reading instruction* (3rd ed.). New York: Longman, 1984.

Pearson, P. D. (2008). *Powerful learning: What we know about teaching for understanding.* San Francisco: Jossey-Bass

Perez, K. (2008). *More than 100 brain-friendly tools and strategies for literacy instruction.* Thousand Oaks, CA: Corwin Press.

Put Reading First. (2000). *The research building blocks for teaching children to read.* Center for the Importance of Early Reading Achievement (CIERA). Washington, DC: U.S. Department of Education.

Radius, M. & Lesniak, P (1988). Student Success Teams: Supporting Teachers in General Education. Sacramento, CA: California Department of Education.

Raphael, T. E., & Au, K. H. (2005). QAR: Enhancing comprehension and test taking across grades and content areas. *The Reading Teacher, 59,* 206–221.

Raphael, T. (1986). Teaching question answer relationships, revisited. The Reading Teacher (39) 6, 516–522.

Rashotte, C. A., Torgesen, J., & Wagner, R. (1997). *Growth in reading accuracy and fluency as a result of intensive intervention*. Miami: International Dyslexia Association.

Rasinski, T. V. (2004). *Assessing reading fluency*. Honolulu: Pacific Resources for Education and Learning. Available at www.prel.org

Richards, T. (2000). Project IV: Functional brain imaging of reading and writing disabilities. University of Washington Learning Disabilities Center, National Institute of Child Health and Human Development.

Riding, R., & Grimley, M. (1999). Cognitive style and learning from multimedia materials in 11-year children. *British Journal of Educational Technology, 30*(1), 43–59.

Ross, J., & Schultz, R. (1999). Can computer-aided instruction accommodate all learners equally? *British Journal of Educational Technology, 30*(1), 5–24.

Shaywitz, S. (2003). *Overcoming dyslexia: A new and complete science-based program for reading problems at any level*. New York: Alfred A. Knopf.

Silverman, L. K. (1989). The visual-spatial learner. *Preventing School Failure, 34*(1), 15–20.

Slavin, R. (1983). When does cooperative learning increase student achievement? *Psychological Bulletin, 94*(3), 429–445.

Slavin, R. (1989). Research on cooperative learning: An international perspective. *Scandinavian Journal of Educational Research, 33*(4), 231–243.

Slavin, R. (2006). *Educational psychology: Theory and practice*. Boston: Allyn & Bacon.

Southall, M. (2009). *Differentiated small group reading lessons*. New York: Scholastic Press.

Southwest Educational Development Laboratory (SEDL). (1997). How can research on the brain inform education? Available at www.sedl.org/scimath/compasss/v03n02/1.html

Spear-Swerling, S. L., & Steinberg, R. J. (1996). *Off-track: When poor readers become learning disabled*. Boulder, CO: Westview Press.

Stone, J., & Kagan, S. (1994). *Cooperative learning & language arts*. San Juan Capistrano, CA: Kagan Cooperative Learning.

Tomlinson, C. A. (2001). *How to differentiate instruction in mixed-ability classrooms* (2nd ed.). Alexandria, VA: Association for Supervision and Curriculum Development.

Torgesen, J. K. (1998). Catch them before they fall. *American Educator, 22* (1 & 2), 32–39.

Uhry, J. K. (2005). Phonological awareness and reading: Theory, research, and instructional activities. In J. R. Birsh (Ed.), *Multisensory teaching of basic language skills* (2nd ed., pp. 83–111). Baltimore, MD: Brookes.

Vaughan, J., & Estes, T. (1986). *Reading and reasoning beyond the primary grades*. Boston: Allyn & Bacon.

Vincent, A., & Ross, D. (2001). Learning style awareness. *Journal of Research on Computing in Education, 33*, 1–10.

Wade, S. (1990). Using think alouds to assess comprehension. *The Reading Teacher, 44*(7) 442–451.

Wang, M. C., Reynolds, M. C., & Walberg, H. J. (1995). Serving students in the margins. *Educational Leadership, 52*, 12–17.

Wasik, R. A., & Slavin, R. E. (1993). Preventing early reading failure with one-to-one tutoring: A review of 5 programs. *Reading Research Quarterly, 28*, 179–200.

Wolfe, P. (2001). *Brain matters: Translating research into classroom practice*. Alexandria, VA: Association for Supervision and Curriculum Development.

Woodward, A., & Elliott, D. (Eds.). (1990). *Textbooks and schooling in the United States*. Chicago: University of Chicago Press.

Worthy, J., & Broaddus, K. (2001). Fluency beyond the primary grades: From group performance to silent, independent reading. *Reading Teacher, 55*, 146–151.

Zwiers, J. (2004). *Building reading comprehension habits in grades 6–12: A toolkit of classroom activities*. Newark, DE: International Reading Association.

Index

About the Author

Dynamic presentations that are meaningful, memorable, and motivational! kperez@stmarys-ca.edu

Dr. Kathy Perez, an award-winning classroom teacher, administrator, and author, has worked with students of all ages, from preschoolers to college graduates. Dr. Perez is currently a Professor of Education at Saint Mary's College of California, Director of Teaching Leadership, and Coordinator of Professional Development and Outreach. A dynamic presenter and "teacher cheerleader," she has the experience to captivate and motivate her audiences.

Kathy is an acclaimed international educational consultant, author, and motivational speaker, specializing in instructional strategies and creative approaches to literacy, learning, and leadership development. She integrates state-of-the art methods and research with passion and practical insights from her own classroom experiences. In her entertaining and thought-provoking sessions, she forms a powerful connection with her audiences.

Dr. Perez has extensive teaching experience as a general educator, special educator, literacy coach, and curriculum and staff development coordinator. Even the most reluctant learners are engaged through her techniques!

Teachers from all grade levels and subject areas rave about Kathy's dynamic approach to teaching. Her innovative and interactive workshops are loaded with teacher-tested materials and activities you can use immediately and share with others. Kathy's workshops provide a lively and informative day of hands-on and minds-on learning. Participants learn from an experienced and informed educator who knows *firsthand* the daily instructional challenges of classroom teachers. Her enthusiasm is infectious!

Dr. Kathy has worked extensively with teachers, administrators, and parents throughout the United States, Canada, Europe, Caribbean, Africa, New Zealand, Australia, Hong Kong, and Singapore. Her best-selling books include *More Than 100+ Brain Friendly Tools and Strategies for Literacy!* (Corwin Press) and *Co-Teaching Book of Lists: A Practical Guide for Teachers* (Jossey-Bass).

Her presentation will be like *none* you have ever heard—not only highly educational, but also memorable and meaningful!